How the Church lost The Truth…

… and how it can find it again

Steve Maltz

**SAFFRON
PLANET**

Saffron Planet
PO Box 2215
Ilford IG1 9TR
UK
T: +44 (0) 208 551 1719
E:contact@saffronplanet.net

ISBN 978-0-9562296-1-8

Typeset by **documen**, www.documen.co.uk
Cover design by Phil Maltz
Printed in the United Kingdom

Contents

Acknowledgements

This book is dedicated to all of you good people who have read my books over the past few years and have encouraged me to keep prodding away at the margins and exploring uncomfortable areas.

Special mention must go to my wonderful wife, Monica, who, with her down-to-earth wisdom and endless encouragement, has helped me more than anyone in crafting this book into something that can really speak into the hearts of folk like me and her.

However, this book has been written with one particular person in mind, someone who believes that an enquiring mind is all we have and that all we see around us can be explained through exercising it. Hopefully there will now be a rethink.

Introduction

How the Church lost the Truth? Are you kidding? *Now you're going too far this time*. Are you telling me that the Church doesn't have the Truth and that we Christians are just a deluded bunch of optimists (or pessimists, depending on your theology!) running around in our crazy little world, totally detached from reality? Some of us maybe, but more of them later.

Perhaps I should qualify my statement first. The Church has not lost *all* of the Truth. If it had then we'd all be in deep trouble, unsure of our salvation or our relationship with God and living without any sure hope. The central truths of our Christian faith have come to us intact, though they have had a rocky journey, as you will discover. But there are other truths that have not fared so well in their journey and we shall uncover their story too.

If the Bible is the Word of God, why is it apparently such a complex book to figure out with so many interpretations, understandings and misunderstandings? Have you ever wished that it was all a lot simpler? That you could know the definitive biblical answers to every problem and question? That you could go to a Christian conference and find everyone agreeing about everything? That we wouldn't need the services of theologians and Biblical scholars to tell us what to believe? That we could have a simple uncluttered faith? Yes, that's my dream, too.

I read somewhere that "Jesus is not a theologian but the despair of theologians". How interesting. Of course he came that we may have life, not that we may have systematic theologies, but that is not enough for the army of Christian scholars who have followed him and struggled to understand him. In the *Dictionary of Major Bible Interpreters* there's an alphabetical list of all recognised Bible interpreters. The list runs to 637 names and, intriguingly, not one of them seems to be Jewish. And assuming that all 637 had something unique to contribute, to warrant their inclusion, then we have at least 637 viewpoints on the Bible and as many ways for us mere mortals to understand it.

That's an awful lot of brainpower and hot air! Is this part of God's plan for us? Did He provide us with this unique, wonderful, life-affirming Bible just as fodder for the analytical skills of intellectuals to argue about, or are there ways that simple souls without theological degrees can learn from it, understand it and apply it to our lives? In other words, how do we really get into it?

Do you see my point? Whether you are a seasoned Christian or a casual searcher, when someone tells you to *look it up in the Bible*, it's easier said than done. Where do I start? To a total beginner it can be a daunting task. To some, used to the simple scan of a paperback, this arcane structure of books, chapters and verses can be culture-shock and off-putting in the extreme. Even to the experienced Bible reader, without the help of a commentary or an index it can still be a chore to find relevant sections, let alone conduct a fully blown Bible study.

Yet many have opened the Bible and found all sorts of things; in fact it has been used to justify just about anything.

Those into violent struggle have looked at the Book of Exodus and have seen their struggle and their physical salvation reflected there, rather than by anything Jesus did for them. Then there are those who claim that there is a progressive refinement in God's message as we work our way through it, from Old Testament to New Testament, then into history, believing that Scripture "would adapt itself" on certain issues, with new revelations. The two areas of discussion favoured by these people are the role of women and the treatment of homosexuals. Needless to say this is favoured by the feminist and gay Christian movements. Then there are the "prosperity teachers" who figure out that the patriarch Abraham must have been materially very rich, which means that we must strive for the same, as our Christian right.

I spent a very significant 15 minutes in front of my satellite TV the other evening, watching the Christian channels. Believe me, these 15 minutes would be sufficient to shock any fair-minded Biblical Christian and provided every justification I needed for writing this book. What I saw was beyond parody, because no satirist could have dreamt up such a concentration of the darker and flakier side of Christianity in the media in our country today. Here is a small snapshot:

A charismatic Catholic teacher was telling a packed audience that Scripture alone is insufficient to follow God. An aged and highly influential "prophet" was recounting a story of his meeting with two "beings" (not angels, mind, so what else does that leave?), who introduced him to his dead mother and declared that women are going to take over the Church. A sweating preacher was encouraging his followers to pray blessings over their handkerchiefs, so that they can be sent for healing, deliverance and promotion of prosperity. Another "prophet" was declaring a whole wave of new revelations that will change the way that we see the effects of sin. A highly influential British teacher was theatrically speaking on areas of Christian conduct that owed far more to medieval superstition than the Bible. I am sure that, if I had remained watching, many more vignettes would have unfolded. And I haven't even started on the prosperity teachers!

Are these folk correct in their interpretations and, if not, who says so? The limitations of our culture dictate that we really do need a helping hand when reading the Bible. It was not meant to be this way, but that's where we find ourselves today. For folk living in Bible times it was different. Any written material was scarce or totally unavailable. Parchments and manuscripts were the norm, but each only held a portion of Scripture and these tended to be in places of worship. Our 1st Century equivalent had some, most or all of Holy Scripture in their head. Depending on age, background and sex, it would have been memorised to a certain degree, from just a few key verses to the whole shebang! With brains uncluttered with The Simpsons, CNN and the wit and wisdom of vacuous celebrities, there was plenty of room in there for God's Word! Putting a modern-day Bible in the hands of a 1st Century Jewish believer would probably have provoked the following response: "*it really ain't necessary, I know most of that stuff anyway.*"

So the uncomfortable fact is that, when it comes to the Bible, we need guidance and the problem is that there's a lot of it about! If you're a Christian you go to your pastor or spiritual leader, but then you need to ask where they got their guidance from. If you're not a Christian then who is going to be warning you away from fringe religions, cults and major heresies, who all have their particular take on the Bible? At some point we are going to have to rely on somebody. So, who?

I'm afraid that this book cannot answer that question and, if it did, wouldn't you be suspicious? *Where's he coming from? What's his theology? What's his background? Has he been to seminary or Bible College? Is he Reformed? Is he a Messianic Jew intent on dragging us back into The Law? What's his game?!*

The fact that you are (hopefully) asking these questions is what this book is all about. What we are going to do is ask more questions ourselves and go far deeper than you've ever imagined and what we're going to find there is going to amaze you, intrigue you and empower you. Trust me on this.

There are some issues in the Church that have been a thorn in its side since almost the very beginning. These are important doctrines that have brought such major divisions between Christians that many folk either pay lip-service to them or ignore them entirely. Think of the Church as a body. Yes, I know it's the Body of Christ, but I'm thinking of an earthier metaphor here, an *actual* body. It is my contention that there is a deep sickness in this body, a subtle disease that has crippled its ability to rise to its full potential. As a "doctor" I look for symptoms to give me clues as to what is going on and by analysing each symptom in turn I can arrive at a total picture of what is ailing my patient, so that I can start thinking of treatment.

We are going to look at five symptoms of what is ailing the Body of Christ and these are going to give us pointers to the deep sickness. Switching metaphors, these symptoms now become *battlegrounds* in the context of this book. Five key battlegrounds have existed since the beginning of Church history and the battles are still raging.

The battlegrounds are, as follows: Creation, Israel, Salvation, Hell and End Times.

◊ Creation – were there really six literal days?

◊ Israel – a prophetic or rejected entity?

◊ Salvation – is Jesus really the only way to God?

◊ Hell – is it really as bleak as we are told?

◊ End Times – how are things going to be wrapped up?

We start our story with those who lived within the pages of the Bible, to see what it was like living as people of God's Word, and how pressures from outside were to lend their influences to God's people. Then we are shown a glimpse of how the very first Church still provides the ideal for us to strive for.

Then we'll embark on a tour of Christian history, from the early Church to modern times. It will be a selective tour rather than an exhaustive one, and we will concentrate on the armies and their weapons, rather than the battlegrounds themselves. Without such a grounding, the battles themselves would be a mystery, so it is worth persevering through this middle section of the book (though a convenient summary is provided).

Finally, onto the battlegrounds themselves and the battles fought there. Two things are worth noting now and will be repeated later on. For each battleground:

1. What was Jesus' own understanding of the issues?

2. If Christians have deviated from this, what has influenced them to do so?

It is going to be a revealing and provocative journey into how the Church lost the Truth, but it is an important one, because what is at stake is our understanding of God's revelation to mankind.

However, before we start our journey, here's something to think about...

Prologue

There is a strange man called Theodore Dusty. He lives outside a small village in Wiltshire in a community that he has built up over many years. He surrounds himself with like-minded folk who follow his teachings. There are about 150 of them and they are mainly Polish, with a smattering of Lithuanians and even a family of Fijians. Most of them are skilled carpenters, joiners and metalworkers, either by trade or training, and the community prospers by offering their skills to the surrounding villages, from odd jobs to major construction projects. The rest of them are farmers.

Theodore calls his group *The Fish People* and they are totally committed to him, despite his strange and mysterious ways. He insists that each give him a day's work every week on a project so secret that all have signed non-disclosure contracts, with threats of excommunication. Then there is his insistence on being at the birth of every new baby. Finally, there is the weather station he had built in a shed in the centre of their commune.

All of this would have been of no interest at all, except for a curious fact reported recently on page eight of the local newspaper. Apparently Theodore was last seen rushing out of the house of a Polish family, after witnessing the birth of their son, feverishly blowing on a ram's horn. This had stirred up the whole commune who immediately followed him, first to the weather station, where he made a short speech, then off into the woods. According to the newspaper they have not been seen since. No explanation was given

or fuss made, which is not surprising, considering the headline
of the short piece read, "Fish folk flee ..." and was in a column
reserved for quirky stories and joke items.

As of the time of writing this, Theodore and The Fish People
have not yet re-appeared.

PART ONE

BIBLE YEARS

Where we visit the Good, the Bad and the Ugly, in terms of man's understanding and interactions with the God Who had created them. The Good represents God's words of instructions to His first covenant people. The Bad gives us a glimpse of the "other side of the coin", of the competing worldviews that surrounded them. The Ugly is what happened when the two met.

Then we are reminded of the most exciting time in Church history, the very beginning, where we meet the people of The Way.

The Good...

How can a young man keep his way pure? By living according to your word. I seek you with all my heart; do not let me stray from your commands. I have hidden your word in my heart that I might not sin against you. Praise be to you, O LORD; teach me your decrees. With my lips I recount all the laws that come from your mouth. I rejoice in following your statutes as one rejoices in great riches. I meditate on your precepts and consider your ways. I delight in your decrees; I will not neglect your word.
(Psalm 119: 9-16)

We start with a heavy lump of Old Testament. How can the psalmist be so delighted with rules and regulations? With words and commands, with laws and statutes and precepts and decrees? Aren't we, after all, people of grace, of freedom, of liberty? Who needs laws anyway, hasn't Christ freed us from all of that?

Thus ends a potted summary of the Old Testament all too typical in Christian circles today. It's sad really and all a matter of perception. Perhaps what the Old Testament needs is better public relations, a Bible-bashing P.R. guru with ecclesiastical connections. But, rather, what Christians need is a balanced view of the Bible that views the Old Testament as more than a dusty and outdated old tome. Consider the implications of Paul's words:

These things happened to them as examples and were written down as warnings for us, on whom the fulfillment of the ages has come.
(1 Corinthians 10:11)

There are real lessons for us Christians within the pages of the Old Testament. And what about this?

Is God the God of Jews only? Is he not the God of Gentiles too? Yes, of Gentiles too, since there is only one God, who will justify the circumcised by faith and the uncircumcised through that same faith. Do we, then, nullify the law by this faith? Not at all! Rather, we uphold the law.
(Romans 3:29-31)

Following Jesus does not mean jettisoning what came before him. There is sufficient value in the Old Testament, particularly the Torah, the "law", for it still to be upheld. What this implies has become a long-running and passionate debate if we focus on particulars, such as the dietary laws, so instead we will examine generalities and look at the whole thing in its entirety.

What is the Torah and where did it come from?

There is a Jewish legend that tells of God considering which people He was going to give His teachings (Torah) to. These people would hereafter be bestowed with great responsibilities as God's ambassadors, so He had to get this decision right. First He went to the pagans, the Gentiles, who turned Him down point blank. Then He went to the Edomites who refused it, because they couldn't handle the prohibitions against killing. The Ammonites and Moabites had trouble with the adultery clause and also turned Him down. The Ishmaelites had issues over robbery and the Canaanites couldn't give up their cheatin' ways! All the nations of the World refused the Torah. So God then turned to the Jewish nation...

This takes us to Mount Sinai a few millennia ago. Two Jews are leaning against a palm tree, two out of around three million, impatiently awaiting the return of their leader, Moses, who had ascended the mountain to meet with God...

Do you think he's coming back?
He always comes back – we don't get rid of Moses that
easily. And anyway, he did tell us to wait until he got back.
But thirty eight days! Without food!
He's speaking with the Lord, I'm sure food won't be an issue.
I hear some are talking about bringing back the old gods.
The gods of Egypt! Didn't Moses defeat them... the plagues,
you know?
Even as we speak Aaron is smelting down some gold and
making a golden calf.
Is this an image of the Lord?
Some say. Others say it's Hapi, the bull god of the Egyptians.
Oh dear...

Moses' brother, Aaron, the High Priest for the Children of Israel, was sincere, but wrong ... sincerely wrong. And stupid. Can you believe his pathetic excuse when confronted by a furious Moses?

So I told them, Whoever has any gold jewelry, take it off.' Then
they gave me the gold, and I threw it into the fire, and out came
this calf!
(Exodus 32:24)

Aaron escaped judgement, but three thousand perished. It is fair to say that this whole episode provided a defining moment in Biblical history. It was Satan's last throw of the dice before the official birth of the Nation of Israel, when Moses again climbed Mount Sinai and returned with the Torah inscribed on new stone tablets (having smashed up the first ones in anger).

Then the LORD said: "I am making a covenant with you. Before all your people I will do wonders never before done in any nation in all the world. The people you live among will see how awesome is the work that I, the LORD, will do for you. Obey what I command you today. I will drive out before you the Amorites, Canaanites, Hittites, Perizzites, Hivites and Jebusites. Be careful not to make a treaty with those who live in the land where you are going, or they will be a snare among you. Break down their altars, smash their sacred stones and cut down their Asherah poles. Do not worship any other god, for the LORD, whose name is Jealous, is a jealous God."
(Exodus 34:10-14)

The Torah had been transferred from the mind of God to the world of mankind and things were never to be the same again.

Without the Torah, mankind would have remained rudderless, the only instructions from God having been the set of rules given to Noah, as listed in Genesis 9. They proclaimed that one was now allowed to eat meat unless it contained blood, murder now demanded a reckoning and procreation was to become a priority. Food, death, sex – good for starters, but perhaps not enough for the wise government of a civilised society.

The Torah is best summarised by the instructions found within the first five books of the Bible, in particular the Book of Deuteronomy, which is a summary of the legal elements of it. Although at least these legal elements seem to have been given at Mount Sinai, much of the content of the five books is historical material and would also have been provided as word of mouth from generation to generation over many hundreds of years.

From the Torah we are told:

◊ that God created the World in six days

◊ that Adam and Eve were ejected from the Garden of Eden

◊ that the sacrifice of an animal was now required to ensure God's favour

◊ that Noah and his family were the only ones to survive the Flood

◊ that Abraham's faith in God was to cement him as the founder of a great dynasty

◊ that Abraham's dynasty spent four centuries as slaves in Egypt

◊ that Moses was used by God to liberate this dynasty

◊ that the dynasty, the Children of Israel, became a Kingdom of Priests as a result of their covenant with God at Mount Sinai

◊ that the Children of Israel now had a fixed set of rules, the Torah, by which to live holy, wholesome and acceptable lives

◊ that there were the seeds of an expectation of a future prophet.

I will raise up for them a prophet like you from among their brothers; I will put my words in his mouth, and he will tell them everything I command him. If anyone does not listen to my words that the prophet speaks in my name, I myself will call him to account.
(Deuteronomy 18:18-19)

It is clear that this concept stayed in their psyche for generations to come, because the Jews at the time of Jesus spoke of this person.

After the people saw the miraculous sign that Jesus did, they began to say, "Surely this is the Prophet who is to come into the world."
(John 6:14)

They identified Jesus as the Prophet of whom Moses spoke. Jesus himself didn't seem to disagree, when he spoke these words.

If you believed Moses, you would believe me, for he wrote about me.
(John 5:46)

Let us now revisit Mount Sinai. But first we can sample the atmosphere of this unique occasion in human history, by reading what the writer of the Book of Hebrews had to say of it, by way of a comparison between the Old and the New:

You have not come to a mountain that can be touched and that is burning with fire; to darkness, gloom and storm; to a trumpet blast or to such a voice speaking words that those who heard it begged that no further word be spoken to them, because they could not bear what was commanded: "If even an animal touches the mountain, it must be stoned." The sight was so terrifying that Moses said, "I am trembling with fear."
(Hebrews 12:18-21)

Consider this scene. It is unprecedented in history. It is the foundation of both Judaism and Christianity, so it is possibly the most misunderstood, lampooned and vilified single event ever.

*It's a boiling hot day, early summer in the Sinai wilderness.
Around three million people, men and women, young and old
are standing at the foot of the mountain, looking upwards.
From dense smoke covering the mountain comes first a loud
trumpet sound then a voice, the very voice of God.*

What followed was the Ten Commandments, which God later inscribed on the stone tablets. Think of how special these are. The first Person to speak them was God Himself. The first Person to write them down was also God Himself.

Did this really happen? It either did, or it didn't. We are people of faith. It doesn't mean that we have switched off our brains, it's just that we have learned to not only believe in God, but to trust Him too. If we struggle with this event, or with any similar event in the Bible, then we can choose to disbelieve it. Many have chosen this path. The alternative approach is to *believe it*. Now I did say, believe it and by that I mean *really* believe it, not half-believe or believe it in a way that explains the event in a way to satisfy one's rational brain. Because the plain truth is that, if we believe that the Bible is God's book for us, then we should accept that every word has been endorsed by God Himself and if He says that three million folk heard His voice at Sinai, then that's what happened. To disbelieve it or explain it away as an error, exaggeration or an allegory, is basically calling God a liar. That's putting it strongly, but it really is time to get real with God and His word.

There is a saying that history repeats itself. This is mostly true, but three exceptions particularly come to mind: the fall of Adam, the redemptive sacrifice of Jesus, and God speaking to three million people at Sinai. All are one-off events that have never been duplicated, the first two for obvious reasons. As for the third, it must have been an awesome event, oh to have been there! Three million were there and that's what separates Judaism (and, by extension, Christianity too) from every other religion. It's the only religion that came from *national* revelation rather than personal revelation. God spoke to three million people, not to a solitary Mohammed or Buddha, who had *unverifiable* personal experiences. Now one man could get it wrong, but three million...?

Think about this in another way. If God hadn't spoken to the Children of Israel, or personally given the Torah, the teachings and instructions, to Moses, then the whole framework of Judaism, the whole language and mechanism of salvation, would never have been given to mankind and Christianity would never have taken hold, because this new faith was built on the foundations of the old.

Jesus the Messiah didn't appear in a vacuum, but into a religious framework built around those very teachings and instructions given to Moses. If they had never been given to Moses, or they had not been of divine origin, then the concept of Messiah would have been dead in the water. How could we need a Messiah if we didn't understand what we needed to be saved from, or what mechanism – the shedding of blood – God has chosen to use to allow us to get right with Him? Sinai had to have happened, as an actual event, otherwise our faith would be in vain!

That's how important the Torah is. That is why this chapter is called "The Good". That is why the Psalmist was able to say:

How can a young man keep his way pure? By living according to your word. I seek you with all my heart; do not let me stray from your commands. I have hidden your word in my heart that I might not sin against you. Praise be to you, O LORD; teach me your decrees. With my lips I recount all the laws that come from your mouth. I rejoice in following your statutes as one rejoices in great riches. I meditate on your precepts and consider your ways. I delight in your decrees; I will not neglect your word. (Psalm 119: 9-16)

But this is not a story with a happy ending for those who lived in Bible times. We shall see why in the next chapter.

The Bad
and the Ugly

While God was building up His people with a set of instructions to keep them healthy in body and soul and protecting them with a hedge of stern warnings, the enemy, the devil, was also building up his own people.

We read of his endeavours from the earliest times, with the Nephilim, the "heroes" of old, men of renown, who ensured that the wickedness of mankind had risen to such a level that a flood was needed to filter it out. But the craziness continued and, within a few generations, men were building a tower as a symbol of their pride and ambition, stopped only by a bout of babbling, followed by a good old scattering.

While God was building up His people from the clans of Abraham, the enemy was doing the same with the folk that surrounded them. He sent out his minions to spread confusion and wickedness to these people, black hearted demons masquerading as "deities".

And who were these "deities"? We will focus on just four of them, the ones that appear most frequently in the Old Testament, all of Babylonian origin. The most familiar is *Baal*, or Ba'al. What does the Bible think of this pagan god?

While Israel was staying in Shittim, the men began to indulge in sexual immorality with Moabite women, who invited them to the

sacrifices to their gods. The people ate and bowed down before
these gods. So Israel joined in worshiping the Baal of Peor. And
the LORD's anger burned against them. The LORD said to Moses,
"Take all the leaders of these people, kill them and expose them
in broad daylight before the LORD, so that the LORD's fierce anger
may turn away from Israel."
(Numbers 15:1-4)

This Baal had influenced many Israelites while they were still
wandering around, not quite ready to enter the Promised Land – you
can see why and you can judge the severity of the sin by looking at
the severity of the punishment.

Once the Israelites had been exposed to Baal, they frequently
erected altars to this god, from the times of the Judges, until the
prophet Samuel put a stop to it. Then came the kings, and Ahab
was the first to restart this loathsome practice. By that time, Baal
worship was rife in Israel – you'll remember Elijah's challenge to
King Ahab.

Now summon the people from all over Israel to meet me on
Mount Carmel. And bring the four hundred and fifty prophets
of Baal...
(1 Kings 18:19)

A cult that could boast 450 prophets was serious business, although,
of course, no match at all for Elijah, the only prophet of God left
at that time. The demonstration on Mount Carmel proved to Israel
exactly which God was in charge!

Yet Ahab's own son, Ahaziah, turned to Baal worship and was
to die painfully in his bed for his troubles. Baal worship was to be
eliminated again in the land a few years later by King Jehu, only to
be sanctioned a few years later in the southern kingdom of Judah,
by King Manasseh.

So what did Baal have to offer that the Lord God, King of
the Universe, couldn't the God who covenanted with Israel as

His special people and who rescued them from slavery in Egypt, sustained them in the wilderness and provided them both victory over their enemies and a land of milk and honey to settle in?

Well, for a start, there were a lot of them. There was the Baal of Peor, Baal-Berith and Baal-Zebub for instance, and the Bible often refers to them in the plural, as localised tribal gods. But sometimes the Bible just referred to the single Baal, one deity that lorded it over the others as the head of a hierarchy, with a whole mythological back-story, which I won't delve into here. But let's be honest and just call them demons, for that's what they were, with Satan himself at the top of the infernal tree.

But the real attraction to a people living out there in the elements, who thirsted when it didn't rain and starved when the crops failed, was that the Baal was promoted as the rain god, responsible for the rainy and dry seasons. You can imagine the secret repressed thoughts of those Israelites. *Look, the Lord God does give us all we need, but it doesn't harm us having a bit of insurance on the side. And we have to eat, don't we?*

As Baal worship involved the sex act, through sacred prostitution, this may have been an attraction for some, though this would have opened them to the dangers of the magic rituals, punishable by death according to the Laws of God. Also many of the "holy days" for Baal worship seemed to coincide with those designated for worship of God Himself. So Satan was clever indeed in the way he enticed folk away from the true God, using confusion and counterfeit.

The second "deity" in our hall of horrors is *Asherah*, the goddess, also referred to as the "queen of heaven", as in this verse from Jeremiah, where the prophet, speaking for God, shows extreme displeasure:

Do you not see what they are doing in the towns of Judah and in the streets of Jerusalem? The children gather wood, the fathers light the fire, and the women knead the dough

*and make cakes of bread for the Queen of Heaven. They
pour out drink offerings to other gods to provoke me
to anger.*
(Jeremiah 7:17-18)

Moses made it very clear where he stood with this pagan goddess:

*Break down their altars, smash their sacred stones and burn
their Asherah poles in the fire; cut down the idols of their gods
and wipe out their names from those places.*
(Deuteronomy 12:3)

Who was Asherah? Actually it's not clear, but these poles of
hers were a constant problem. Apparently these were wooden
poles connected to worship of the goddess (a practice, I have
heard, that still continues in some sleazy city nightclubs).
Suffice to say, they were centres for pagan worship and we even
read that King Manasseh had not only carved one out himself
but had it installed in the Holy Temple in Jerusalem. This was a
dangerous and provocative act. God was not to be mocked and
this must have sealed His decision to exile the people of Judah
from the land.

The third "deity" was *Ashtoreth* (Astarte), the goddess of the
Sidonians. Solomon was quite partial to this one, the moon-goddess
and companion of Baal, introduced to him by a good number of his
one thousand wives and concubines.

*As Solomon grew old, his wives turned his heart after other gods,
and his heart was not fully devoted to the LORD his God, as the
heart of David his father had been. He followed Ashtoreth the
goddess of the Sidonians...*
(1 Kings 11:4-5)

The fourth and final "deity" was the very nasty *Molech* (Moloch),
the detestable god of the Ammonites, according to the Bible.

Do not give any of your children to be sacrificed to Molech, for
you must not profane the name of your God. I am the LORD.
(Leviticus 18:21)

Nasty, nasty, nasty. Can you imagine anything worse than child
sacrifice? King Manasseh obviously had no problem with this.

He sacrificed his sons in the fire in the Valley of Ben Hinnom...
(2 Chronicles 33:6)

What on earth could the people have received in return for this
detestable act? Is anything worth this kind of sacrifice?

Moloch's post-Bible career took him to the pages of John
Milton's Paradise Lost, as one of Satan's chief angels and also
to Fritz Lang's ground-breaking film Metropolis, as a term
of horror.

So, on the one hand we had the people of God, the Children
of Israel, a people sealed by covenant and protected by a wall
of love called the Torah. On the other hand we had everyone
else, outside God's covenant and prey to the machinations of the
devil, through his four proxy rulers and other minor "deities".

Never the twain shall mix? Not so; this is where it gets ugly.

The seeds of the downfall of God's people had already been
planted back in the days of Judges, the days of Joshua and Caleb.
The Children of Israel, as instructed and helped in every way by
the Lord God, took the land of Canaan and made it theirs, dividing
the land up among themselves after conquering the nations who
preceded them.

But not all were totally destroyed; some of the Canaanites were
to be allowed to live, usually as slaves. This was going to be a
challenge for God's people, as Joshua himself explained, just before
his death:

Be very strong; be careful to obey all that is written in the Book of the Law of Moses, without turning aside to the right or to the left. Do not associate with these nations that remain among you; do not invoke the names of their gods or swear by them. You must not serve them or bow down to them. But you are to hold fast to the LORD your God, as you have until now. The LORD has driven out before you great and powerful nations; to this day no one has been able to withstand you. One of you routs a thousand, because the LORD your God fights for you, just as he promised. So be very careful to love the LORD your God. But if you turn away and ally yourselves with the survivors of these nations that remain among you and if you intermarry with them and associate with them, then you may be sure that the LORD your God will no longer drive out these nations before you. Instead, they will become snares and traps for you, whips on your backs and thorns in your eyes, until you perish from this good land, which the LORD your God has given you.
(Joshua 23:6-13)

He lays it all out for them. He reminds them of their unique status as God's people. How could they want it any other way? The people respond:

Then the people answered, "Far be it from us to forsake the LORD to serve other gods! It was the LORD our God himself who brought us and our fathers up out of Egypt, from that land of slavery, and performed those great signs before our eyes. He protected us on our entire journey and among all the nations through which we traveled. And the LORD drove out before us all the nations, including the Amorites, who lived in the land. We too will serve the LORD, because he is our God."
(Joshua 24:16-18)

The people responded, *of course we will follow the Lord. We're not crazy, we know what's good for us!* But Joshua knew better, he knew his people; so he gave them some home truths:

> *Joshua said to the people, "You are not able to serve the LORD. He is a holy God; he is a jealous God. He will not forgive your rebellion and your sins. If you forsake the LORD and serve foreign gods, he will turn and bring disaster on you and make an end of you, after he has been good to you."*
> (Joshua 24:19-20)

This could be a comedy moment, perhaps from a Mel Brooks film. You could imagine the people shuffling uncomfortably, twiddling their thumbs, avoiding eye contact with Joshua. *Of course we will serve the Lord!*

Joshua persevered and pushed the point further.

> *"You are witnesses against yourselves that you have chosen to serve the LORD."*
> *"Yes, we are witnesses," they replied.*

Still shuffling awkwardly, eyes darting to the left and the right, nervous whistling. Then Joshua hits them with a thunderbolt.

> *"Now then," said Joshua, "throw away the foreign gods that are among you and yield your hearts to the LORD, the God of Israel."*

The correct response would have been, *yes we will throw them away. We'll just fetch them now while you prepare the bonfire.* Instead their response is perhaps a bit flat, robotic and insincere. There seems to be no record of the "foreign gods" being thrown away.

> *And the people said to Joshua, "We will serve the LORD our God and obey him."*

Joshua gave them the benefit of the doubt and made a covenant with God on their behalf at Shechem, but he must have been groaning inwardly.

Joshua died before things started to go badly wrong. We are shown this at the start of the book of Judges. The Israelites still had more fighting to do before they could fully claim the land. They met a determined foe and weren't able to drive out all the Canaanites, so kept them as slaves instead. What followed was the biggest shift in God's relationship with the Israelites since the Covenant was given on Mount Sinai all those years earlier.

God appeared to them, in person, as the angel of the Lord and spoke:

> *I brought you up out of Egypt and led you into the land that I swore to give to your forefathers. I said, 'I will never break my covenant with you, and you shall not make a covenant with the people of this land, but you shall break down their altars.' Yet you have disobeyed me. Why have you done this? Now therefore I tell you that I will not drive them out before you; they will be thorns in your sides and their gods will be a snare to you.*
> (Judges 2:1-3)

Joshua had judged them correctly, they were not 100% God's people, they had been swayed by the gods of the vanquished Canaanites who were living with them. God is simply telling them, *you've made your bed, now go and lie on it!*

The story of the Israelites is basically all downhill from that day onwards. Why were they so easily swayed? Hadn't God proved Himself to them so many times in word and deed? What was the matter with these people?

But, then again, we could say… what's the matter with us, too? How many of us Christians, when we have seen God working so mightily and graciously in our lives, have granted Him ever decreasing influence, as we forge our way through life. It's a very human failing, so there's no point blaming those early Israelites.

Instead we should all band together... and blame Adam and Eve, who got that particular ball rolling.

A tiny seed was to multiply. To see its full effect we must return, around 800 years later, to King Manasseh of Judah. And what a horror he was!

Firstly he rebuilt the high places, the hilltops where pagan gods were worshipped counterfeits of the only divinely sanctioned high place, the Temple in Jerusalem. This is not worship as we know it, but rather animal and human sacrifices, prostitution and the practice of the dark arts. The centre point would have been sacred pillars, carved with the likenesses of the pagan gods and goddesses and considered as dwelling places for these "deities".

So King Manasseh, descendant of King David, had dragged the kingdom down through his worship of this detestable crew of pagan entities. If that wasn't bad enough, he also worshipped the stars in the night sky, giving them individual altars in the Temple. He also practiced sorcery, divination, witchcraft and consulted mediums and spiritualists.

And the people of the Kingdom of Judah themselves were just as bad:

But the people did not listen. Manasseh led them astray, so that they did more evil than the nations the LORD had destroyed before the Israelites. (2 Kings 21:9)

Oh how God must have dealt with Manasseh. Surely he had earned the death penalty a hundred times over? God had smitten others for far less crimes.

Manasseh was taken prisoner by the Assyrians, who shackled him, shoved a hook through his nose and dragged him off to Babylon. *Go for it, justice at last*, we cry. But what's this...?

In his distress he sought the favor of the LORD his God and humbled himself greatly before the God of his fathers.
(2 Chronicles 33:12)

At this I exclaim in "righteous anger", *some hope! Come on God, just give him both barrels!*

And when he prayed to him, the LORD was moved by his entreaty and listened to his plea; so he brought him back to Jerusalem and to his kingdom. Then Manasseh knew that the LORD is God.
(2 Chronicles 33:13)

What?! I cry.
Deal with it! God responds.

Who says that the God of the Old Testament can't be the God of the New Testament because He is not merciful? You simply can't get more forgiving and merciful than this!

But enough about Manasseh. He had a son, Amon, who had plenty of opportunity to assess his father's career. This he did and decided to take the "evil pills" and, because he refused to see the light, was killed by his own officials. He left a son, Josiah, a king to confound the psychologists, neither following the dark ways of his immediate forbears, nor relaxing in the rut of power and privilege. He had started the much-needed reforms in the land, ten years earlier at the age of 16. Needless to say, the people of Judah were already doomed, a people ripe for judgement.

Although King Josiah *did what was right in the eyes of the Lord*, these acts were to save him but not the nation. His sons turned out to be a bad lot, which mattered not, as theirs was the generation that was exiled to Babylon. God's judgement could not be forestalled any longer and, we are told in the starkest possible way that God's anger against Judah and Jerusalem was such that:

...in the end he thrust them from his presence.
(2 Kings 24:20)

Exile followed, then a return, albeit to a land suffering under foreign occupation. We now move ahead a few hundred years, to the time of the Romans and to the time of Messiah Jesus.

The Way
of the Truth

*Don't you know that a little yeast works through the whole batch
of dough? Get rid of the old yeast that you may be a new batch
without yeast—as you really are.*
(1 Corinthians 5:6,7)

Yeast puffs up and affects all that surrounds it. It is a picture of
spiritual pride and arrogance. But there is now a new way, Jesus
Christ. He is absolute perfection, totally lacking in this old yeast
and we are asked to follow likewise.

*For Christ, our Passover lamb, has been sacrificed. Therefore let
us keep the Festival, not with the old yeast, the yeast of malice
and wickedness, but with bread without yeast, the bread of
sincerity and truth.*
(1 Corinthians 5:7-8)

During the Passover meal he identifies with the bread without
yeast, the unleavened bread, the *matzoh*, although most
Christians (except, curiously, the Catholics), when sharing the
bread of Communion, choose to do so with *leavened* bread,
matzoh with added extras. It is these "extras", these additions to

the pure faith of the apostles, that have caused such damage to the Church since the early days, and why Christianity still walks with a limp.

In a sense the earliest Christians, the apostles and their followers from the Book of Acts, were to start life in much the same way as the Children of Israel, the Jewish Nation. Each were provided with the Truth, from the finger of God at the time of Moses and from the Son of God Himself for the Church. In both cases things were to go wrong as a result of the pure message being polluted by the yeast or leaven of pagan worldviews.

Oh, how things could have been so different! We move to the early pages of the Book of Acts.

There they stood in the first glimmer of twilight, eleven men who would change the World. Eleven men, shivering in the evening chill, in that olive grove on that hilltop overlooking the Holy Temple of Jerusalem. The twelfth, also shivering, but different. He was the one who had died and then risen.

After all, Jesus had appeared to them regularly over the last 40 days, teaching them, instructing them, mentoring them. The Eleven had so much to learn in so little time, important things that each would spend the rest of their lives teaching others, in Jerusalem and in all Judea and Samaria and to the ends of the Earth. And that time had just come to an end.

The last question Jesus had to answer was delivered by Simon, also known as the zealot.

"Lord, are you at this time going to restore the kingdom to Israel?"

Jesus addressed his answer to the whole group.

"It is not for you to know the times or dates the Father has set by his own authority. But you will receive power when the Holy

Spirit comes on you; and you will be my witnesses in Jerusalem,
and in all Judea and Samaria, and to the ends of the earth."
(Acts 1:7-8)

Three voices responded in unison. Each was cut short by what
happened next. Eleven men held their breath, their eyes slowly
arcing heavenwards as Jesus ascended to Heaven.

Suddenly a voice, a deep textured voice, startled them back to
reality. Two men, dressed in white, were standing before them and
were speaking in unison.

"Men of Galilee, why do you stand here looking into the sky?
This same Jesus, who has been taken from you into heaven, will
come back in the same way you have seen him go into heaven."

You could have heard a pin drop, eleven men in complete silence,
shock and bewilderment. They were by now quite used to
unusual occurrences, but this one had a finality to it that gave an
uncertain assurance.

Jesus had gone, they were on their own now, armed with the
memories and teachings of the divine man who had walked with
them for three years. Soon another divine helper, the Holy Spirit,
was going to appear on the scene to empower them for the task of
preaching the Truth to the world that surrounded them.

Here they were, every one of them a Jew brought up under
Roman occupation. All were, to various degrees, students of the
Holy Scripture, more so now that Jesus had opened them up to
ways that combined old wisdom with new understandings.

In one sense he had changed nothing. After all, hadn't he said:

"Do not think that I have come to abolish the Law or the Prophets;
I have not come to abolish them but to fulfill them."
(Matthew 5:17)

Mostly, it wasn't actually a case of Jesus changing anything, it was more a case of realignment, of demonstrating the true meaning of the Torah, the Holy Scriptures, stripped of the interpretations added to them by teachers, however well-meaning.

Just as the Israelite settlers in Canaan had to turn from the pagan ways they were exposed to by the indigenous Canaanites, and the Jews of the Kingdom of Judah had to rid themselves from the same influences that had, ironically, been re-introduced by their own rulers, so the apostles had to filter out the human influences from the divine instruction.

These human influences went by the name of the Oral Law. This was supposedly given to Moses at Sinai, at the same time as the written Torah, as a commentary on it. It was then passed down from person to person, never written down until long after the time of the apostles.

So the Pharisees and teachers of the law asked Jesus, "Why don't your disciples live according to the tradition of the elders instead of eating their food with 'unclean' hands?" He replied, "Isaiah was right when he prophesied about you hypocrites; as it is written:
" 'These people honor me with their lips, but their hearts are far from me. They worship me in vain; their teachings are but rules taught by men.' You have let go of the commands of God and are holding on to the traditions of men." And he said to them: "You have a fine way of setting aside the commands of God in order to observe your own traditions!"
(Mark 7:5-9)

As it was at the time of Isaiah, so it was at the time of Jesus... and so it is now, too. Whether you are an orthodox Jew reading from the Talmud, or a Catholic priest with his Catechism, or an Anglican with his Book of Common Prayer, you are doing your religious duties with the help of a set of man-made traditions, even if they are inspired by or contain Holy Scripture within their pages.

The question to ask is whether the human additions are useful embellishments or disguised distractions. Do they draw you nearer to God and His purposes for your life, or further away? We will return to this question later.

The apostles and disciples had sat at Jesus' feet for three years, finished off by a 40 day concentrated crammer. Now the Master was gone and, for now, they were alone. It was as if Jesus had painted his thoughts, ideas and teachings on blank slates. Each of them had made a clean break with the past and all theology and doctrine would be as received at the feet of the Master.

If Jesus declared – which he did – that Hell was a place of eternal punishment, where there is gnashing of teeth and where the fire never goes out – then that's how it was. No question, no debate, no objections borne out of human reason or sense of fair play. *Turn or burn* may not have actually come from the mouth of Jesus, but the idea was his and his apostles accepted this without question.

He was similarly clear cut about many other things. For instance, he was extremely well placed to have a view about the creation of the universe, the world and mankind. Actually *being* there at the beginning tends to focus your outlook, after all!

He is the image of the invisible God, the firstborn over all creation. For by him all things were created: things in heaven and on earth, visible and invisible, whether thrones or powers or rulers or authorities; all things were created by him and for him. He is before all things, and in him all things hold together.
(Colossians 1:15-17)

So Jesus was both the means and reason for Creation. The very same person who had eaten, talked, laughed and cried with the apostles over the previous three and a bit years had witnessed the awesomeness of the *beginning* of beginnings. It is so hard to take that in, but it's true!

"It was because your hearts were hard that Moses wrote you this law," Jesus replied. "But at the beginning of creation God 'made them male and female'."
(Mark 10:5-6)

The beginning of Creation suggests that man appeared near at the start, say six days in, rather than after billions of years of chance mutations. Yes Jesus was not just the Creator, but also, by extension, a Creationist.

So, at this point of history, the apostles and early disciples were pioneers of a new tradition, teachings direct from God Himself. They went by the name of "the Way" and we read of their activities in this much-quoted passage right at the start of the story of the Church, in Acts 2:

They devoted themselves to the apostles' teaching and to the fellowship, to the breaking of bread and to prayer. Everyone was filled with awe, and many wonders and miraculous signs were done by the apostles. All the believers were together and had everything in common. Selling their possessions and goods, they gave to anyone as he had need. Every day they continued to meet together in the temple courts. They broke bread in their homes and ate together with glad and sincere hearts, praising God and enjoying the favor of all the people. And the Lord added to their number daily those who were being saved.
(Acts 2:42-47)

Is this not one of the most exciting passages in the Bible? A people transformed from an uncertain rabble to those devoted to the apostles' teaching, to fellowship, to the breaking of bread and eating together in their homes and to prayer.

And they also had time to meet every day in the temple courts, in full view of the people in the most provocative way, in the holiest place, the Temple area. In today's terms it would be like having our prayer meetings and services in our shopping malls, museums, or council chambers – our "holy places".

What else did they do?

All the believers were together and had everything in common. Selling their possessions and goods, they gave to anyone as he had need.

All the believers were one in heart and mind. No one claimed that any of his possessions was his own, but they shared everything they had. With great power the apostles continued to testify to the resurrection of the Lord Jesus, and much grace was upon them all. There were no needy persons among them. For from time to time those who owned lands or houses sold them, brought the money from the sales and put it at the apostles' feet, and it was distributed to anyone as he had need. Joseph, a Levite from Cyprus, whom the apostles called Barnabas (which means Son of Encouragement), sold a field he owned and brought the money and put it at the apostles' feet.
(Acts 4:32-37)

Is there a church today that can truly say that it is fully duplicating all of these activities listed, in an atmosphere of freedom, liberty and openness?

We read later in Acts what effect the Way had in the world around them.

... if he found any there who belonged to the Way, whether men or women, he might take them as prisoners to Jerusalem.
(Acts 9:2)

But some of them became obstinate; they refused to believe and publicly maligned the Way...
(Acts 19:9)

About that time there arose a great disturbance about the Way.
(Acts 19:23)

So the Way was causing a disturbance, being publicly maligned,
and some were even thrown into prison. They were also a church
of great power.

*The apostles performed many miraculous signs and wonders
among the people. And all the believers used to meet together in
Solomon's Colonnade. No one else dared join them, even though
they were highly regarded by the people. Nevertheless, more and
more men and women believed in the Lord and were added to
their number. As a result, people brought the sick into the streets
and laid them on beds and mats so that at least Peter's shadow
might fall on some of them as he passed by. Crowds gathered
also from the towns around Jerusalem, bringing their sick and
those tormented by evil spirits, and all of them were healed.*
(Acts 5:12-16)

Miraculous signs and wonders in public! The sick being laid in the
streets for healing and deliverances. *All of them were healed!* Is this
not real revival? Give me some of this old-time religion!

But they were starting to cause a disturbance. The religious
leaders were not happy. We read of this in the very next verses
in Acts:

*Then the high priest and all his associates, who were members
of the party of the Sadducees, were filled with jealousy. They
arrested the apostles and put them in the public jail. But during
the night an angel of the Lord opened the doors of the jail and
brought them out. "Go, stand in the temple courts," he said, "and
tell the people the full message of this new life." At daybreak
they entered the temple courts, as they had been told, and began
to teach the people.*
(Acts 5:17-21)

When you have God's favour, nothing can hold you back! More became believers – even priests became Christians – the equivalent of today's scientists or radical politicians becoming believers.

It wasn't to last. The enemy was most unhappy.

On that day a great persecution broke out against the church at Jerusalem, and all except the apostles were scattered throughout Judea and Samaria.
(Acts 8:1)

The Church began its journey… into the nations, forced out by persecution – rather than by missionary zeal. Isn't that interesting?

And this is where the *real* problems began.

PART TWO

CHURCH YEARS

Where we zip through the history of the Western Church. It's not an exhaustive tour with key dates, personalities and movements, but rather it's an examination of what influences came in from the outside and what effect they had on the Church.

As important as it is for you to appreciate the historical forces that have shaped today's Church, some of you may find the following four chapters fascinating but heavy-going. And heaven forbid you should give up on the rest of the book on account of being bogged down by the unfamiliar. So here's what I have done for you. Read this section and if, in all honesty, you start thinking – hey, didn't I give up this sort of stuff at school? My brain hurts – then skip to chapter 8, entitled "to cut a long story short", and you will get a short summary on what you've missed. Not the most satisfactory way of reading this book, but, as the key messages are in the second half of this book, I don't want you to miss them through getting lost in the woods.

Plato's Playground

"The most unkindest cut of all." Even Shakespeare, who penned these words, would have winced at what was happening in this darkened room in the City of Alexandria in Egypt, early in the 3rd Century AD. Origen, perhaps the most famous Christian philosopher of his day, was both offender and victim in this act and, as he sliced away, this troubled man was consoled by the thought that at least he wouldn't be a danger to the women that he was instructing in the faith.

There's a huge irony in this act. You see, Origen had castrated himself as a literal interpretation of Matthew 19:12: *"For some are eunuchs because they were born that way; others were made that way by men; and others have renounced marriage because of the kingdom of heaven."* He believed that he was serving God in this painful and needless sacrifice. Yet this was the same Origen who was bringing into the early Church a whole new way of reading the Bible, techniques gleaned from Greek philosophy that frowned very much on literal interpretations of Scripture.

There's a huge leap there from the gentle self-control advocated by the apostle Paul to this brutal self-castration. Yet Origen, who knew his Hebrew and Greek Scriptures, had made an informed decision that was utterly wrong. How could this be? How could a man with responsibilities as a teacher, in his role as principal of the

School of Alexandria, read Holy Scripture in such an extreme way? To help us here we need to follow the movements and growth of the early Church, once it had left the pages of the Book of Acts.

The two towering figures of Acts, Peter and Paul, were dead, martyred at around the same time in Rome. A few years later, only John, of the original apostles, remained. After suffering exile on the Island of Patmos, he ended his years in Ephesus. He was quite ancient by then and a man of great renown. After all he was not only the last surviving witness to Jesus in the flesh, but was also one of the Messiah's closest friends. It's no wonder that eager young Christians flocked to sit at his feet and learn from this mighty apostle.

One such man was Polycarp, who John himself ordained as Bishop of Smyrna. Here was a man eager to continue the witness of John. He had memorised many of John's eyewitness accounts of Jesus' miracles and teachings and was proud of his association with the apostle. He lived a life dedicated to the teachings of the apostles, a pure witness and a much needed witness, because changes were afoot. Heresy had arrived and Polycarp met it head-on in a visit to Rome at around 154 AD.

The Christian heretic was Marcion. His ideas were wrong but heavyweight enough to wreak havoc for centuries to come, and Polycarp was annoyed enough to declare him *the firstborn of Satan*. These ideas were the first whiff of the anti-Judaism that was going to infect the Church in later years and Polycarp would have none of it. In fact, after ensuring the excommunication of Marcion, his next task was to try and stop the Roman Church from dumping the celebration of the death and resurrection of Jesus according to the Hebrew calendar. All he was doing was trying to preserve the Biblical traditions of the original apostles. Unfortunately, he was to fail in this worthy task and met his end shortly afterwards, one of the first Christian martyrs.

The legacy of Marcion, known as *Marcionism*, was the first great assault on the pure faith of the apostles. Here was a man so heavily influenced by the Greek philosopher, Plato, that he was willing to allow these pagan ideas to create a wedge between the Old Testament *of the Jews* and the New Testament *of the Christians*. Plato believed in *dualism*, a separation between the spiritual and the physical, the former being "good" and the latter "evil" (more of this in my previous book, *How the Church lost The Way...*).

Marcion took this dualism and applied it to the Bible. He reasoned that the Old Testament represented the failed religion of the Jews, supplanted by the spiritually-charged New Testament of the Christians. He also rejected the nasty, wrathful, "*God*" of the Old Testament, in contrast to the forgiving God of the New Testament. In his dualistic thinking, the people (the Jews) and the god (Yahweh) of the Old Testament represented the evil physical world and the people (the Christians) and the God (Jesus) of the New Testament represent the good spiritual world.

To Marcion, Paul was the only apostle worth considering and chose Luke as the only reliable gospel. But he didn't leave it there. As the gospel of Luke contains many Scriptures at odds with his dualistic views, he got out his scissors and snipped away. Out went all references to the Old Testament, such as the nativity narratives, in fact out went the first three chapters entirely! So, in *his* "gospel", Marcion presented to his followers a Jesus with absolutely no back story!

How on earth did Marcionism survive? It was clearly a case of trying to fit a square pagan peg into a round Biblical hole and, when it didn't fit, to hack away at the hole with a chisel. Yet survive it did and we are going to see it emerge again and again as we follow our story through the pages of history.

Another Church Father of note was Ignatius, a friend of Polycarp and, with all probability, another disciple of the apostle John. One Catholic "holy legend" claims that he was the child who Jesus took into his arms with the words, "*whoever welcomes one of these little children...*". Ignatius became the Bishop of Antioch, the place where, in the Book of Acts, the name *Christian* first started to be used for followers of Jesus. Ignatius was eventually martyred in Rome early in the 2nd Century AD, writing a series of letters at the end of his life that addressed matters of doctrine and practice.

The third and final figure from the early days with a link to Biblical history was Clement of Rome, one of the early popes. His claim to fame was supposedly as the "Clement" mentioned by Paul in Philippians.

Yes, and I ask you, loyal yokefellow, help these women who have contended at my side in the cause of the gospel, along with Clement and the rest of my fellow workers, whose names are in the book of life.
(Philippians 4:3)

Clement wrote a letter to Corinth, known as the First Epistle of Clement, considered the oldest Christian letter outside the pages of the New Testament, a letter full of knowledge and understanding, filled with the deeds of characters from both Old and New Testaments. Here was a man who'd evidently been to countless Bible studies, rather than philosophy classes.

And so we come to the end of what is known as the Apostolic period. Now all who had known Jesus had died, as had those who had known those who had known Jesus. The Church was now on its own, but how was it going to cope? Was it going to move forwards guided by direct instructions from the letters and gospels of the original apostles and by the oral traditions preserved by those, such as Polycarp, with direct links with the original Church? Or was it going to look around at the World, at deceivers like Marcion, and allow other ideas to get into the mix?

One man, the next Church Father in our historical survey, provided a clue. Justin Martyr was his name, though his life was certainly not defined by the manner of his death. There are three better possibilities – Justin Philosopher, Justin Jew-baiter and Justin Apologist. Justin set the scene for battles yet to come for the heart and soul of the Church.

Justin was born around 100 AD in what was then Palestine. His background was thoroughly Greek and he had been a follower of Plato until a chance meeting with an old guy on a beach who introduced him to Christianity. Justin was converted and regarded Christianity as "the true philosophy", marking him as the first in a long line of *Christian philosophers*, perhaps the saddest oxymoron of them all! Hence *Justin Philosopher*.

He was not entirely a "new creation" when he embraced faith in Jesus Christ and the fact that he chose to dress in the recognised costume of a teacher of philosophy (their equivalent of the dog collar and all the other paraphernalia) indicated that here was a man determined to find a workable mix of faith and philosophy. Impurities added to a quartz crystal can add vivid colour, yet the impurity of pagan thinking that Justin added to the pure teachings of Jesus Christ led to a watered-down message, weak and unreliable. These impure teachings were spread through his writings. One was *The Dialogue with Trypho the Jew*, from which he earns his second honorary title, *Justin Jew-baiter*.

This was an attack on the Judaism of the Jews who had rejected Jesus and were now dispersed through the nations. What started out as gentle reasoning soon gave way to blatant attack and *The Dialogue with Trypho the Jew* was probably the earliest anti-Jewish diatribe produced by the early Church. At a time when unbelieving Jews were very much in opposition, it is most telling to see that many of his arguments were constructed within the framework of the teachings of Plato and Socrates. It is here, in chapter 11, that we read the following:

> *We have been led to God through this crucified Christ, and we are the true spiritual Israel, and the descendants of Judah, Jacob, Isaac, and Abraham, who, though uncircumcised, was approved and blessed by God because of his faith and was called the father of many nations. All this will be proved as we proceed with our discussion.*

The first seeds of replacement theology, the idea of the Church as *Spiritual Israel*, had now been sown by the first major Church Father to have no connection with the original Jewish apostles of Jesus. And these seeds, as we will see, had been sown in soil fertilised by the pagan culture of the day.

Justin dug in the knife in other ways too. There was the claim that the Christians not only had a more accurate translation of Scripture (the Greek Septuagint, which was actually translated from the Hebrew Scripture of the Jews), but understood it better. He also accused the Jews of Scripture twisting and, most incredibly of all, of persecuting Christians – though only as far as telling stories about them or cursing them in the synagogue. So, Justin Martyr was no friend of the Jew and helped to create a theological framework that would be used by future generations to justify their own hatreds.

The final epithet is *Justin Apologist*, the role by which he is best known. An apologist is not someone who *apologises* for being a Christian, but rather defends it. Justin was in a good position to defend the Church against the various heresies, such as Marcionism, that were emerging, because he'd been there and had the t-shirt. Justin knew the vocabulary and mindset of the heretics because their roots, like his own, were in Greek philosophy.

So what heresies are we talking about now? Didn't Polycarp see off Marcion just a few years earlier? The best way of getting a grip of the murky world of heresies is to start with the first encounter with a heretic by the apostles in the Book of Acts.

Now for some time a man named Simon had practiced sorcery in the city and amazed all the people of Samaria. He boasted that he was someone great, and all the people, both high and low, gave him their attention and exclaimed, "This man is the divine power known as the Great Power." They followed him because he had amazed them for a long time with his magic.
(Acts 8:9-11)

This man, popularly known as Simon Magus belonged to that nefarious group that, according to the Old Testament, *provoked the Lord to anger*. He was a sorcerer, he dabbled in the black arts and didn't mind who knew. He was a Jew in open rebellion with his maker, with many followers. Even worse, he claimed to be *the Great Power*, rivalling God Himself. He was treading on dangerous ground.

> *But when they believed Philip as he preached the good news of the kingdom of God and the name of Jesus Christ, they were baptized, both men and women. Simon himself believed and was baptized. And he followed Philip everywhere, astonished by the great signs and miracles he saw.*
> (Acts 8:12-13)

Simon became a believer and was baptised. So, end of story? Not quite. Was there something suspicious about this interest in signs and wonders? Could there have been a selfish motive? Moving on in the story, to verse 18, we read:

> *When Simon saw that the Spirit was given at the laying on of the apostles' hands, he offered them money and said, "Give me also this ability so that everyone on whom I lay my hands may receive the Holy Spirit."*
> (Acts 8:18-19)

He had nailed his colours to the mast! His was no conversion as a response to the preaching of the gospel of Jesus Christ. His was just a lucrative career move. The "Great Power" had witnessed a *greater power* and wanted it and was willing to pay for it.

> *Peter answered: "May your money perish with you, because you thought you could buy the gift of God with money! You have no part or share in this ministry, because your heart is not right before God. Repent of this wickedness and pray to the*

LORD. Perhaps he will forgive you for having such a thought in your heart. For I see that you are full of bitterness and captive to sin."
(Acts 8:20-23)

Suffice to say, Simon did not get his wish and we are not told what happened next.

I earlier called Simon Magus the first heretic. Why? A heretic is someone who rejects or corrupts established doctrines. We can assume that Simon was familiar with basic doctrine; we are told he believed and was baptised. Yet it was clear that, as the so-called "Great Power", his interest was as a collector of *powers*, seeking to add the Holy Spirit to his menagerie of demons, by whom he was carrying out his sorcery. His heresy probably followed on from this episode, promoting teachings combining Christian belief with all the other nonsense he had already picked up on the way. More specifically, Simon Magus became known as not just the first heretic, but the first *Gnostic* heretic. So Gnosticism, the daddy of all heresies, is where we go to first.

Gnosticism is the result of thinking like a Greek and then re-moulding Christianity accordingly. This is implied by the name itself, *gnosis* being the Greek word for "knowledge". Gnostics through history have been puffed-up individuals, just like Simon Magus, who have boasted "secret knowledge", who consider themselves as special superior beings who, through these divine secrets, have ascended to a higher level than mere mortals. The problem comes when others also believe that there is value in following these deluded individuals. We will read more of this later on.

Just like Marcionism already mentioned, Gnosticism was borne from the *dualism* of Plato. Remember Plato's major statement: the spiritual world is good, the material, physical world is bad. Because of this, Gnostics (as with Marcion) believe that the material world was created by a "lesser god" and that Jesus, the "greater god", taught secret knowledge to the "spiritual elite". Gnostics have always been great scribblers and a lot of their early writings have been found, which is a shame!

These were the type of people faced by Justin Martyr, or Justin Apologist, who wrote a series of letters, the apologies, to fight these ideas. Yet he wasn't the "main man" of the early Church; the greatest apologist of that period was *Irenaeus*, the Bishop of Lyons, a disciple of Polycarp.

Irenaeus' best known book was *Against Heresies*, which did what it said on the tin. Its main target was Gnosticism, particularly that practiced by a guy known as *Valentinus*, the best known Gnostic heretic of the 2nd Century AD. Although Valentinus had a large following and wrote much, little of his writings survive. His teachings were classic Gnosticism, mixing teachings from the apostles with the dualism of Plato and ending up with an esoteric system suitable only for the "superior intellects" of the day. Ireneaus dealt with Valentinus' teachings in *Against Heresies* using humour and ridicule. He lampooned his version of Gnosticism in a satire involving gourds, cucumbers and melons.

Docetism was another form of Gnosticism dealt with by Ireneaus. Another dualistic twist, this heresy may seem ridiculous to us, but it was a serious problem at that time. Docetists could not believe that the "spiritual" Jesus could have suffered, wept, hungered, thirsted and died in agony. Consequently, they declared that Jesus only *appeared* to experience these things. This of course is an extreme consequence of dualism and it required them to actually change the verifiable facts of Jesus' life on Earth in order to fit in with their philosophy.

Ireneaus had yet another target in his cross-hairs, a heretic called Montanus. Here was a Christian who "heard voices", claiming them as direct revelations from God and usually travelled around with two women of similar inclinations, one of whom claimed that Jesus had appeared to her in female form. Known as *The Three*, this sorry band created havoc throughout the Christian world of the mid-2nd century AD. They spoke to large gatherings, driving sensible folk into ecstatic excitements on hilltops, waiting for the

Second Coming. Perhaps you can see parallels to some streams of the Church in the 21st century?

Irenaeus knew that this sort of nonsense had to be dealt with otherwise all sorts of misguided individuals were going to start hearing voices and deceiving the masses. He declared that the best way to put a check on these people was to turn to Holy Scripture as authority. The main problem was that the New Testament had not been fully compiled yet, although obviously all the letters and gospels had been doing the rounds of the churches of that day. Irenaeus was instrumental in protecting the early Church from people like Marcion, who were distorting the Word of God, and folk like Montanus, who were trying to add to it!

The focus now moves to North Africa, to the first Church Father to write in Latin. Tertullian was another fierce opponent of the early heretics, putting the boot into Marcion, among others. It is claimed that he hated Greek philosophy, declaring that Plato and others, though freely acknowledged by other Church Fathers, were the forefathers of heretics. This marks him out in my book as one of the good guys in terms of the fight to maintain Biblical purity, though an absolute rotter in terms of his negative attitude to the Jews. Tertullian had a lousy ending; he seems to have become a raving Montanist at the end of his life, conjuring up an image of an aged ascetic letting his hair down, grabbing his robes and dancing off into the sunset, declaring the imminent return of Christ.

Meanwhile in the city of Alexandria, Egypt, in the 2nd Century AD, there lived a man called Clement. He also was a Church father, but oh dear, oh dear, oh dear! My reservations here are because of his conscious efforts to formalise the merging of Christianity and Platonism. As head of one of the most important schools of the day, this was going to have serious consequences. He created a form of Christian Platonism that was to creep into the mainstream Church and affect the key areas of Christian living and Bible interpretation. He did this perhaps for the right reasons – to engage with the Greek culture of his day – but a diluted or corrupt truth is perhaps worse than no truth at all.

Imagine this scenario in a trendy modern church. The minister looks around at his dwindling congregation and decides that the best way to increase numbers is to be relevant to those who live in the neighbourhood. So he advertises movie nights, showing excerpts from feature films. He shows Star Wars. *See the force? That's the Holy Spirit.* Then E.T. *See how he comes back to life? Just like Jesus. Evan Almighty? See, that's how God works.* Imagine you're in the audience, having no prior knowledge. *Where do I sign up? I didn't know Christianity was so cool!* The minister has increased his numbers at the expense of the truth. He has sold them a religion that combines the Christian message with modern culture, but Christianity it ain't!

So Clement took examples of gods from Greek literature and said, *that's just like God.* He examined Greek legends and said, *they're similar to these Old Testament stories, so they share some truths.* He took Plato's philosophic ideas and twisted them to explain Christian themes. He rewrote the Sermon on the Mount in the language of neopythagorean gnomic wisdom, which is definitely all Greek to you and me! In fact he had a lot of ideas on how to re-interpret Holy Scripture. He was not just a Christian philosopher but a *Christian Gnostic.* He considered Christianity the true philosophy and the perfect Christian the true Gnostic. He had somehow made heresy acceptable!

Clement had set the scene for the one who came after him, his most able pupil, Origen the castrati, the man at the head of this chapter. Origen is hugely influential to this day, because his ideas, a natural development from those of Clement of Alexandria, form part of the vocabulary of the Church today, particularly in the field of Bible interpretation. We sniggered at his self-castration, perhaps there's a touch of admiration for the godly zeal that prompted this action, but the damage he did to the Church far exceeded any he did to his parental prospects.

The damage that he did was magnified due to the fact that he was said to have penned around 6,000 works, all publishing costs underwritten by a rich friend. Here is an example. It is the third paragraph of the Preface of his work entitled *De Principiis*:

> *Now it ought to be known that the holy apostles, in preaching the faith of Christ, delivered themselves with the utmost clearness on certain points which they believed to be necessary to every one, even to those who seemed somewhat dull in the investigation of divine knowledge; leaving, however, the grounds of their statements to be examined into by those who should deserve the excellent gifts of the Spirit, and who, especially by means of the Holy Spirit Himself, should obtain the gift of language, of wisdom, and of knowledge: while on other subjects they merely stated the fact that things were so, keeping silence as to the manner or origin of their existence; clearly in order that the more zealous of their successors, who should be lovers of wisdom, might have a subject of exercise on which to display the fruit of their talents—those persons, I mean, who should prepare themselves to be fit and worthy receivers of wisdom.*

This seems to be a claim of biblical insufficiency, that the Bible isn't necessarily the final word. He is stating that the New Testament writers didn't speak clearly intentionally, in order that those who followed – *lovers of wisdom* – could exercise their talents and expand on the ideas within the Biblical texts. In other words the Bible is a free-for-all for any who claim to be *fit and worthy receivers of wisdom.*

This is dangerous and also smacks a little of Gnosticism, which is unsurprising considering that Origen's teacher saw little danger in this. Origen himself wrote commentaries of many of the Old Testament books and was the first to really make consistent use of the Greek technique of *allegory* when he did so. I wrote of this in my previous book and rather than re-invent the wheel, here is the gist of what I said:

In the context of this book allegory is a key concept, so it's worth explaining it in full, in order to fully understand it in every way. It is defined as a way of representing a situation, giving it a meaning that is not a literal meaning. Examples are the best way of getting a grip of this.

George Orwell's *Animal Farm* is an allegory of the Soviet era of Stalin in the pre-war years. Whereas kids may have a hate figure in Napoleon the pig, there is a greater hate figure implied as Stalin himself. So, if we take the story *literally*, it's just a story of talking animals on a farm, but *allegorically* it's a political satire.

The movie *The Wizard of Oz*, gives great joy to kids and adults alike, with its basic homespun philosophy. It also exercised the brains of generations of scholars and commentators who saw allegory throughout. So, in its literal sense, it's just a good kid's yarn, but as an allegory it is mostly seen by economists as a critique of the gold standard, hence the *yellow brick* road.

One big question we need to ask is whether the author intended to create an allegory and, if so, what point is he making? In George Orwell's case, the allegory was clear and unambiguous. With The Wizard of Oz, L. Frank Baum, the author, never made it clear what the real meaning of the movie was.

So what about the Bible? Well, we know the author, God Himself. So when Origen went through the text of the early books of the Old Testament, he had to be sure that, if he saw allegory, then the author Himself would need to be in agreement. And, if He wasn't, then Origen was treading on dangerous ground indeed!

Why would Origen have to use allegory anyway? It's worth returning to Plato's *dualism* and delving deeper to extract the core thinking behind it. When Plato says that the soul is good and the body is bad, he is declaring a basic principle that has many guises. In religious terms, he is saying that the physical world, the one in which we live, is bad (or evil) and the spiritual world (Heaven and such places) is good, and therefore worth striving for.

Because of this, Origen was uncomfortable whenever, in the Bible, God (a spiritual being) mixes with us on a human level (the material world), when He interacts with man personally, or shows human characteristics or emotions. When Origen created his commentaries, he would look beyond any literal interpretations of the verse for deeper meanings, *allegories*. In fact this became a regular feature of his work, looking for deeper "spiritual" meanings behind Bible verses that the author (God) meant just to be taken literally.

A favourite theme of his was to re-interpret the Old Testament in the light of the New Testament, using techniques from Greek philosophy, married with insights from early Christian tradition and other writings. His driving principle was that the Bible contained three levels of meaning, corresponding to the body, soul and spirit. You can see the influence of Plato here, particularly when he adds that the "body" level of meaning, the literal meaning of the text, is for the more simple minded whereas the "soul" and more particularly the "spirit" levels of meaning are for the *more enlightened* readers. If Origen discerned where a Bible passage spoke about Christ, then, for him, this *had to be* the original meaning of the text. This may have come from the noblest of motives, but is it correct, is this what God had in mind when He authored the text?

So where does this broad sweep of the early Church Fathers bring us? One question that it does raise concerns the Bible itself. Isn't it meant to be the complete, authoritative, all-encompassing, infallible and eternal Word of God? Yet we see so many rules, regulations, creeds and doctrines added on by these Gentile Christians in the Greek speaking world. Was it because the Bible wasn't... complete, authoritative, all-encompassing and infallible? Let's allow our minds to drift back...

Let's ask ourselves why the gospel writers bothered, why Paul and Peter wrote those encouraging letters to churches, why John recorded the Revelation of Jesus Christ. They did so because God prompted them to do so. God also made sure that these documents were protected and eventually collated together into the canon of Holy Scripture.

Then came the Church Fathers and others. Some wrote letters, some wrote essays, others even wrote gospels. Yet one needs to ask this: if Holy Scripture was sufficient for our needs, why did we need this extra stuff, from Ignatius of Antioch to Origen of Alexandria? The simple answer is that antidotes were needed for the poison of heresy. Folk were being led astray, false teachings had arrived and were messing people up.

Then we ask this: what was the nature of these heresies that required new writers and teachers to explain them away and point people back to the truth? These heresies were assaults on the mind, which was bad enough but the problem was that, once the mind was convinced as to what was true or false, actions followed. And it is these actions, these practices which flowed from these new doctrines and brought confusion. In addition, they led people on – it has to be said – a fast-track to Hell because they had been kept from the simple message of the gospel of Jesus Christ.

As we have seen, these heresies were generally birthed in the admittedly brilliant but sadly pagan minds of the Greek philosophers of an earlier generation. Unfortunately, the Early Church inhabited a World defined by its Greek culture and, once the Jewish apostles had died, the Church... was... gradually... sucked... in!

This is the crux of a big problem that has had repercussions through to modern times, in terms of Church unity, Bible interpretations and Christian practices. You could say that Christianity was hamstrung before it had even started the race. How was this so?

Heresies were one thing and many people presented different views of God the Father, Son and Holy Spirit and the relationships therein at that time. It was right that the Church Fathers, drawing from their own experiences, countered these aberrations as best they could. But these early teachers too were fallible men and many were throttled by their own training and backgrounds. Most had been exposed, even trained, in Greek Philosophy from an early age and so, when presented with the truths of Holy Scripture, tackled these new revelations with the tools of Greek logic and understanding. Sacred writings birthed within the worldview and language and understanding of Hebrew culture were re-evaluated and re-interpreted in a totally alien way.

It was like using a cheese grater to create mashed potatoes. It was like expecting a brain surgeon to do his stuff wearing boxing gloves. The wrong tools. The Church Fathers and those who followed felt that the Holy Scriptures were not sufficient to give them understanding and that new tools were needed, tools that had been used to dissect the worlds of Homer, or construct a clever rhetoric or classify the World scientifically. These Church Fathers (with the honourable exception of Tertullian and some others who taught in Antioch) proudly called themselves Christian philosophers, but it went further than that. We must remember that one of the key minds of that era, Clement of Alexandria, saw no problem with *Christian Gnosticism*. Heresy had become mainstream! You couldn't even tell the poachers from the gamekeepers!

And it wasn't just about passionate discussions and healthy disagreements. Priscillian, Bishop of Avila, and his followers were beheaded by Church authorities in AD 385 for living and teaching a life in accordance with Scripture, rather than accepting the corruptions of State Christianity. They were said to be the first Christians actually executed by the Church. Sadly, many more were to follow.

We now skip a few generations, to a time when secular society of the known Western world had become Christian, or is it the other way round?

Aristotle's Laboratory

The sun had set on Europe. The light of the World had been dimmed, lost in the shadows in most places. We are near the end of that period, known historically (and controversially if the revisionists are to be believed) as the Dark Ages. It is 920 AD.

So what was the state of the nation in that year? The liberating truth of the gospel of Jesus Christ had been around for nearly nine centuries, plenty of time to clean up a dirty, filthy, corrupt World. But these were the *Dark* Ages, not an optimistic title. What had gone wrong? Where was the evidence of redeemed lives? Where had the light gone? Had Christianity failed, betrayed by the flaws of the human heart, or by external forces that it just couldn't stand up to?

It was a truly sorry picture. The Roman Empire was long gone. Christian Europe had imploded, the true faith torn apart through the corruptions of State Christianity and invasions from the north and the east, forcing migrations and uncertainty. Violence swept the lands, cities destroyed, churches ransacked, agriculture diminished and populations declined, most languishing as peasants or slaves.

Lots of factors have been attributed to this dramatic reverse – plague, the rise of Islam and the Huns and Barbarians, even an ice age in the 6th Century. Not too much is known of this period, due to the lack of active contemporary historians in this turbulent and uncertain time. It seems that people were too busy watching their backs to contemplate their social architecture. And, of course, few could actually write! So we must look inwards, at the Church itself. What were the Christians doing at this time? The Holy Bible had been finalised and distributed centuries earlier, so God's revelation to mankind was available to all. Wasn't this enough to provide all the answers at that time?

Of course it was, if people had access to it or had the necessary skills not just to understand it, but to actually read it in the first place. Literacy was virtually non-existent except with the clergy, the *professional* Christians. Even many kings of the time were illiterate. The common man and woman eked out their existence in a haze of superstition and ignorance.

The Christian dream had become a nightmare. In the last chapter we saw the young Church growing under the questionable guidance of the Greek and Latin Christian philosophers. The issues that concerned them became Church-wide debates at that time, engaging all. Pagan ideas may have infiltrated the Church, but at least there was a passionate dialogue going on, at least brains were thoroughly engaged. Something had happened in the intervening years. If Google had been around at the time, powered by the hot air of Greek rhetoric, popular searches in the year 250 AD could have been: *What is the relationship between Jesus and the Father? What are the beliefs of Montanism? How relevant is Platonism in the Church? Why can't I celebrate Passover with my Jewish neighbour?* Moving along to 920 AD we find our search engine powered by mud, grime and the ash of torched churches. Popular searches could have been: *Why are there so many private parts of St Ananius? How can you ward off a magic charm? Why are monks so fat? Why does my Jewish neighbour need to feed off Christian blood?*

It was a big step from the world of philosophy and reason of the 3rd Century, to the dark places of superstition and irrationality of the 10th Century. To get one insight on this it is worth considering the life and works of probably the most influential thinker of the early Church, Augustine of Hippo. To Catholics of every generation he is one of the most important figures in the development of Western Christianity. To others he is the philosopher who infused Christian doctrine with Platonism, another *Christian philosopher* already!

Augustine was enormously influential in many ways. From him we get the idea of original sin and our traditional understanding of evil. He has contributed much, yet it is worth looking at what influenced him. He was originally a follower of *Manicheanism,* a cult that promoted a form of dualism, with good versus evil, light versus darkness, body versus soul. His later influence was Ambrose, the Bishop of Milan, who introduced him to the Bible interpretation techniques of Origen, developed from the dualistic ideas of Plato.

He wrote a book, *City of God*, as a defence of Christianity against the paganism that surrounded it in the final days of the Roman Empire. Ironically it contained a visible attack on Platonism, but Plato got in his retaliation first as the unseen influence, the invisible director working behind the scenes in the writing of this book.

So how did Plato posthumously pull the strings? It's all down to his "big idea", embedding the falsehood known as *dualism* in the early Christian minds, from Clement of Alexandria, Origen and others, to Augustine himself. It's the idea that the *physical*, material world is bad (or evil) and that the *spiritual*, heavenly world is good and to be eagerly sought. To be blunt, it's a death cult masquerading as a philosophy of life and these early Christian thinkers had a theology thoroughly infiltrated by it.

In the book, Augustine consoled his readers that one should not concern oneself with such worldly matters as the destruction of Rome, the *City of Man*, but should rather look heavenwards at the "city yet to come", the *City of God*, the New Jerusalem of the Book of Revelation. On the face of it this is a noble mission, a thoroughly Christian pursuit, but to measure the true worth of a book is to examine its legacy. What sort of influence did the *City of God* have on those who read it, on those who converted its words into action?

It was a very large book, full of challenging ideas and it was to be read in many different ways, by different people. Some saw the book as a handbook for a *theocratic* society, governed by the Church, or those appointed by it, whether king or pope, as the best way forward. Others took a different view. By holding out hope for the Christian, by saying in effect, *don't worry about the mess in this world you have to live in, there's a better world to come*, many saw, in these words, justification for the acceptance of a life of disappointment, deprivation and disaster as *there's better to come in the next life*! As the publication of this book was swiftly followed by the *Dark Ages*, there's a strong possibility that this seminal book from the most influential Christian thinker in a society that considered itself a Christian one, had something to do with it!

The new kind of Christians, after the fall (of Rome), had little interest in their bodies as such. They cared about the health of their souls. They had no interest in consumption. They could lose their reputation rather than gain it for possessing wealth in a society where poverty was next to godliness. Roman wealth was replaced by Christian poverty. (A History of Knowledge, Charles Van Doren p.96, Ballantine Books 1992)

Just as we, living in the affluent West in the 21st Century, believe that progress is determined by the number of cars in the garage, the size of our plasma screens or the availability of exotic foreign spices in our supermarkets, our 10th Century friends would have considered themselves living in enlightenment, devoting their lives to the well-being of their souls, that precious commodity, their ticket to a good afterlife. In a way, perhaps they got it right! The trouble is that their objective may have been a good one, but the way of getting there was eminently flawed.

Sacraments were the way into Heaven at that time. Ordinary folk couldn't understand a word of the liturgies in their local church, as it was all in Latin. Neither did they have a correct balanced understanding of Jesus, as Bibles were just not available for the common man and, if they had been, no-one would have been able to read them. Yet they were told that if they followed the actions dictated by the sacraments they would be alright. Sacraments controlled their daily lives. Baptism at the start of life was absolutely necessary, as was regular penance – confessing your sins (with payment to the Church) and regular Holy Communion. Real, considered, saving faith didn't come into it. You were "saved" through one's actions, as if the act itself was sufficient. It is a sad and sobering thought to consider how many from those times had a nasty shock in the next world. You must also wonder whether someone with an incomplete, even false, understanding of the historical Jesus and the purpose of his death is any better off than an ignorant native in the heart of the Amazon jungle. Only the Lord has the answer to that one.

But things weren't that bad everywhere. Flames of the gospel were still flickering with the desert hermits, but also in some monasteries. We visit one such place. It is in France. It is the Abbey of Cluny, at that time home to the largest Christian building in the World. In contrast to most monasteries of the day, this one was allowed to operate independently of the state (in the form of its patron, William the Pious), though not of the pope. The Abbey was run by Benedictine monks, following the rules set by this religious order, founded by Benedict of Nursia, in the 6th Century. The original rules of this movement were based around a balanced path of body and spirit, between the needs of the individual and the wider group.

This all had changed by the 10th Century, as the Benedictine movement got richer and more powerful and had swept through all the lands of the Western Church. And with power and money came compromise and corruption. Originally monasteries were populated by monks with a calling from God to serve Him in a structured community of like-minded people. By the 10th Century monks tended to be taken from the ranks of the nobility, as a vacation rather than a vocation. Their nature of work changed as a result, with less emphasis on manual work and more on scholarly and artistic pursuits, holy holiday camps for the privileged, less a religious community and more a secular corporation, fully integrated with the society of the day rather than as isolated working retreats.

Christianity had become so institutionalised that the common person really had no "religious" duties any more, apart from keeping the sacraments. Monks would do everything else. They prayed for you, took penance from you and interceded for your salvation. It was *dualism* gone mad. Every aspect of your religious life was now in the hands of others, controlling you through the sacraments, for the price of a few coins. It was as if the whole monastery movement was now dedicated to St Plato!

Such was the state of the Western Christian Church in the year AD 920. It may have been a "Dark Age" for them, but, not so far away, others were experiencing a *Golden Age*. These were the Jews of Spain living, believe it or not, in a thoroughly *Muslim* environment, under the conditional benevolence of Islamic rulers. So what was going on there?

During the Christian "Dark Ages" Islam was on the move, spreading outwards in all directions from its origins in the Middle East. Its farthest western reach was Spain, ruling it between the 8th and the 11th Century through the Umayyad dynasty. Stability was achieved through the ability of Amir Abd al-Rahman to pull together all rival groups and get them working together in peace, producing a golden age of Islam, with great advances in the areas of the arts, economics, sciences, philosophy, literature and much more. This was good news also for the Jews and Christians living in Spain who, although tolerated as inferior to Muslims, were given certain freedoms. In fact the Jews absolutely revelled in their status, something they had never experienced in Christian society, provoking a flowering of their talents in a period of history known later as the *Golden age of Jewish culture in Spain*.

It may have been a *Golden Age*, but there was a price to pay. His name was Aristotle and a huge price was paid in the area of Jewish theology. According to the Jewish Encyclopaedia:

One thousand years after his death, Aristotle, as his pupil Alexander (the Great) had aforetime done, began to conquer the East, and finally ascended to the supreme rulership of the entire realm of medieval thought.

Wow! That's some legacy for this Greek philosopher, the pupil of
Plato, who had died a few hundred years before Christ. His ideas
were to follow Plato into the realms of Christian theology, as we
will read later. But Judaism was conquered first and it was the
Jews' own fault! The "Golden Age" was not to be a new awakening
of Judaism, but an embracing of the very mindset rejected at such
cost by their forbears over a thousand years earlier at the time of
the Maccabees. *Chanukah was about to be soiled, the pagans had
re-invaded the Temple and this time the menorah's light dwindles
to nothing.*

The year is still 920 AD and we meet one of those responsible
for this development. His name is David al-Mokammez and he was
part of a process that started in the 8th Century, instigated by the
Moslem rulers, for multi-lingual Jews to rescue the writings of the
Ancient Greeks by translating them from the "lost" Greek language
into Arabic and eventually into Hebrew. Among this material was
that of Aristotle, who al-Mokammez named "the philosopher", a
sign of the esteem in which he held him.

As a result of all this, learned Jews were not just those who were
great religious scholars of the Torah and the Talmud, but now started
to excel in the more "Greek" pursuits of astronomy, mathematics,
philosophy and science. They were no longer driven just by a
"Hebraic" zeal for God and all His ways, but a very "Greek" thirst
for understanding of the World around them and what makes it tick.
The teachings of Aristotle had opened up this "Pandora's box", so
to speak, and it has remained open ever since.

Another living at that time was Saadia Ben Joseph, who was
said to be the first Jew to seriously tackle the secular fields
of science and philosophy, despite also writing many Bible
commentaries, Hebrew dictionaries and Jewish liturgies. He could
be said to be a bridge between the two worlds, in much the same
way as Philo of Alexandria who, at the time of Christ, attempted
to bridge the Greek and Hebrew mindsets in his commentaries
on the Old Testament. Just as Philo was Plato's willing Jewish
lapdog, Ben Joseph performed the same function for Aristotle,

adopting the principle that Bible interpretation must not contradict human reason.

Enough already about Aristotle; so what exactly did he teach? Good question but not so easy to answer, as he taught so much. Plato's core teaching of *dualism* can be grasped quite easily in the formula: *spirit = good, physical = bad.* Not so Aristotle. There are no simple formulae, so it's best to rephrase the question. *What was so attractive about Aristotle's teaching for the Jews living under Muslim rule in the 10th Century?*

This is best answered by looking at the Jewish philosopher who became Aristotle's greatest champion. This was Abraham Ibn Daud, who lived in Toledo, Spain about a century after Saadia Ben Joseph. He was considered the first *Jewish philosopher*, rather than a philosopher who just happened to be Jewish. This is an important distinction. Let's say he was the first Jew with stated profession of "philosopher" on his passport.

Ibn Daud saw philosophy explaining certain matters that Scripture was silent about. He was bothered when Rabbis failed to agree about issues such as free will and just saw philosophy as a new tool in the armoury of interpretation, making use of human reason alongside divine revelation. In his book, *The Exalted Faith*, he first introduces Aristotle to his Jewish audience, covering natural science and the order of the universe, then seeks to interpret Judaism in the light of this new knowledge. So, using Aristotle to examine the basic principles of the nature of being (ontology), physics, theology and astronomy, he tackles five basic principles of Judaism, namely: the source of faith, the oneness of God, divine attributes, God's actions, and prophecy. After examining each with the tools of philosophy, Ibn Daud found Scriptures to back up his findings, in such a way as to affirm his use of Aristotle in Bible interpretation.

So Ibn Daud was using the philosophy of Aristotle to *tear God apart and see what is inside.* No longer was faith and trust sufficient for the restless mind, even God himself was not beyond the disciplines of logical scientific analysis. This view is a long way from the simple faith of their forefathers Abraham and Moses.

But there were others in the Jewish world who trod a more traditional path. The year again is 920 AD, the place is Tiberias, in Palestine. Whereas al-Mokammez, Saadia Ben Joseph, Ibn Daud and others were to allow pagan pollutants into Judaism, Rabbi Aaron Ben Asher was doing his best to protect the very bedrock of their faith, the Holy Scriptures of the Old Testament (the Hebrew Bible).

The last of a venerable family of scribes known collectively as the Masoretes, their mission since the 7th Century was to create a system to fix the pronunciation, structure and even musical notation for the Hebrew Scriptures and, by doing so, help to preserve the integrity of the words themselves. Christians and Orthodox Jews to this day have a lot to thank these scholars for. One such set of Ben Asher's manuscripts, known as the *Aleppo Codex*, has survived a turbulent history to find a home in the Shrine of the Book museum in Jerusalem. It is said to be the oldest and most complete Hebrew Bible in current existence.

Ben Asher was an interesting man and not without his enemies. His greatest opponent was, in fact, Saadia Ben Joseph, our philosopher. And the reason for this opposition is an interesting one. It appears that Ben Asher was a member of a Jewish sect, known as the *Karaites*. Although this didn't stop the Jewish world in general from accepting his work as valid, Ben Joseph took great exception to this. He simply hated the Karaites.

The Karaites are better described as a movement rather than a sect, but you try telling that to Orthodox Rabbis! Their name means "readers of the Hebrew Scriptures" and they were fundamentally a *back to basics* movement, recognising only Holy Scripture, the *Tanakh* (Old Testament), and nothing else as their religious authority. No wonder Saadia Ben Joseph considered them a sect, as the Karaites rejected the Oral law, the Talmud and all such writings as authoritative.

For someone who devoted his life to the Holy Scripture, it is not hard to see why Ben Asher embraced this movement. It is also not hard to understand Saadia Ben Joseph's opposition to it. Ben Joseph also had a reverence for Holy Scripture, but added to that were the "traditions of the Elders", whether familial, as in the Talmud of the Jewish sages, or alien, as in the writings of Aristotle and other Greek philosophers.

And here we come to a vital point, affecting Jews and Christians alike. It's that word *tradition*, brimming with cosiness and nostalgia, but full of hidden danger. It implies respect for one's elders and forbears and provokes the feeling that *if it was good enough for those who came before me, it should be good enough for me*. This is how it works. You start with a set of central truths agreed by all, then, as time goes by, layer upon layer of opinion, interpretation and commentary are added on, like volcanic strata covering a central core. You eventually arrive at a point where the core, the central truth, is so hidden from view, so divorced from the action, that it just becomes a memory.

Rabbinic Judaism, the most orthodox religious expression of the Jewish faith and historical enemy of the Karaites, has added so much "tradition" to the central truths of the Tanakh (Old Testament) that God's Word is muffled. But what of the Christian denominations, particularly the historical ones like the Roman Catholics and the Greek Orthodox? What we find is that these Christians have far more in common with Rabbinic Judaism than they would care to realise or admit.

The Rabbis boast a continuous line tracing back allegedly to Moses and his oral law, with countless branches of commentary, representing the various sages and their followers. The Catholics prefer more of a linear approach, with pronouncements from the popes of history to quash any potential budding from the main trunk. But in both cases, the party line for doctrine and practice are the human commentaries, rather than the Word of God, as if the divine mind was just providing *discussion starters*, as raw material to be mulled over and improved upon by theologians throughout history.

We will now meet three key thinkers, divided by religion but united in other ways.

A Jew, a Christian and a Muslim...

No, this is not the beginning of a joke, but real history and very important history it is too.

We start with the Muslim. We know him as *Averroes*, though his full name was Abu 'l-Walid Muhammad ibn Ahmad ibn Rushd. He was one of the cleverest men living in the 12th Century, excelling in philosophy, theology, law, logic, psychology, politics, medicine, astronomy, geography, mathematics and physics. He created a school of philosophy and has been described as *the founding father of secular thought in Western Europe*. He was very big on Aristotle and his commentaries on the Greek philosopher were very much a bridge between ancient philosophy and the Jewish and Christian philosophy of his day.

He lived in Cordoba in Spain, where the "Golden Age" mentioned in the last chapter was still running strong. Interestingly his writings made little impact on the Muslim world but, once his work was translated into Latin, his fame spread to the Christian world, even earning him a place in Dante's Inferno, as the author of the *great commentary*. In fact, for many scholars centuries afterwards, Averroes was known as *the* Commentator.

Living also in Cordoba, at the same time, was a man who was henceforth to be known as the most important Jewish thinker for centuries. His name was Moses Maimonides and such was his output that it was later said that "if one did not know that Maimonides was the name of a man, one would assume it was the name of a university". Known also as *Rambam*, an acronym for **Rabbi Moses ben Maimon**, he was the first person to gather together all Jewish law into one place, the *Mishnah Torah*. He was also a Jewish philosopher and, for Christians, will always be remembered by his major work, *The Guide to the Perplexed.*

Maimonides was the latest and greatest of the line of Jewish philosophers that began when Saadia Ben Joseph first dipped his toe into the works of Aristotle a century or so earlier. He now also had the thoughts of the Muslim philosopher, Averroes, to work with and proved himself a master of synthesis, creating out of this a form of *religious rationalism*. This, as we will see, will be the outcome of mixing up Holy Scripture with Aristotle. The Word of God is now going to be prodded and dissected using the tools of Greek philosophy, just as it was at the time of the Church Fathers. In those earlier times, the alien influence came from Plato, resulting in a skewed understanding of God's ways from the dualism that separated the physical and the spiritual.

The Christian world is now going to be similarly impacted by Aristotle's influence and it's not going to be a pretty sight. Which brings us to the last member of our triumvirate... the Christian.

Surely we are in good, safe hands for someone once known as the "dumb ox", on account of his size and demeanour. But don't let that fool you; as a contemporary of his said, "you call him a dumb ox; I tell you that the Dumb Ox will bellow so loud that his bellowing will fill the world." And so it did.

His name was Thomas Aquinas, an Italian, and he was to become the most important and influential Christian philosopher of the Middle Ages. Again we see the unholy amalgam, *Christian philosopher,* and realise that if this guy was so influential then the whole concept of Christian philosophy was well and truly in the mainstream. And he was true to his title because Thomas dedicated his life to the use of Aristotle's rationalism in Christian theology, influenced greatly by Maimonides the Jew and Averroes the Muslim.

Here is his big idea, which was to provide a break from existing views. He said that *the things of God and the human soul can be understood not just by divine inspiration but also through human reasoning from what could be sensed from the World that surrounds us. Also the existence of God is not to be taken as a given (i.e. through faith) but through analysis of information that can be gathered through the senses.*

In other words he proposed a marriage between faith and reason. A good example of this is his Five Ways, his five "proofs" for the existence of God, human reason encroaching on the territory usually occupied by faith. Here they are in a nutshell:

First Way: Everything that moves must have been moved by something else and the very first *mover* must have been God. This is expanded to include the "potential" for something to become something else, needing something from outside itself to get the process started. Again this chain goes back to God. This showcases God as the *Great Sustainer*.

Second Way: Everything in this World has a cause behind it and this cause itself is caused by something else. We call this the law of *cause and effect*. If we take this right back we arrive at the *prime causer*, God.

Third Way: Everything in the World exists, putting it simply, or has *contingent existence*, putting it not so simply. Everything exists because something existed before it. Taking this back we again arrive at God, without Whom nothing would exist. Confused? I certainly am.

Fourth Way: Every person in the World has a morality somewhere on the scale between goodness and badness. For *goodness* to have some meaning there must be the ultimate goodness, which is God, the most perfect Being and the Source of all goodness and perfection.

Fifth Way: Every object in the World must have got there because something else had the intelligence to create it. This is the argument for intelligent design, with God as the *Designer*.

Alternatively you can just have faith in God, with no need for the mental gymnastics of deductive reasoning.

Now faith is being sure of what we <u>hope</u> for and certain of what we do <u>not</u> see.
(Hebrews 11:1)

By contrast, reason could be said to be pretty sure of what we've just figured out and certainly *not* sure of anything that we *can't see*. The word *reason*, interestingly is derived from the Greek word, *logos*, which gives us "logic", translated into Latin as "ratio", giving "raison" in French, which translates as "reason" in English. Of course *logos* is also identified as Jesus in John 1, the means by whom all things are made. It's best not to go there right now, that's a whole book in itself (in fact it's discussed in the first chapter of my book, *Jesus, Man of Many Names*).

So what's all this about *reason*? Is this a new concept in the life of man, a secret in our collective consciousness, unlocked by the rediscovery of Aristotle? Did Jesus use reason? What does the Bible say?

The most relevant mention is here:

"Come now, let us reason together," says the LORD. "Though your sins are like scarlet, they shall be as white as snow; though they are red as crimson, they shall be like wool."
(Isaiah 1:18)

Yet even here it is God and man reasoning together. A better understanding of the Biblical approach is here:

Now the Bereans were of more noble character than the Thessalonians, for they received the message with great eagerness and examined the Scriptures every day to see if what Paul said was true.
(Acts 17:11)

Rather than using their mental faculty to figure God's Word out using the tools of logic, the Bereans simply examined the Scriptures. Their first course of action was to look at God's Word, rather than looking within themselves. That is a *Hebraic* action, as distinct from a Greek one. Faith comes from revelation that comes from God's Spirit working through God's words to illuminate the mind, rather than conclusions and deductions brought about by human reasoning, even if it is God's words that are being pored over.

In a way of a summary of all we have learned in the last three chapters, here is a good way of understanding what the Greeks, whether Plato or Aristotle or others, gave to the development of Christianity. Let us pick the most representative expression of the first three key periods of God's dealing with mankind; Old Testament times, New Testament times and the Early Church. The Old Testament is represented by the Ten Commandments, the New Testament (for sake of argument) is represented by the Sermon on the Mount and the Early Church gave us the Nicene Creed, the longest lasting expression of Christian faith.

Two of these are connected, the other one stands out like a sore thumb. The first two concern themselves with conduct, how we should live our lives. Belief in the giver of these commandments and declarations is a given, it's not an issue.

Honor your father and your mother, so that you may live long in the land the LORD your God is giving you.
(Exodus 20:12)

Blessed are the poor in spirit, for theirs is the kingdom of heaven.
(Matthew 5:3)

And here is the start of the Nicene Creed, formulated in AD 325 by the first ecumenical council meeting in Nicea, in Turkey.

We believe in one God, the Father Almighty, Maker of all things visible and invisible. And in one Lord Jesus Christ, the

Son of God, begotten of the Father [the only-begotten; that
is, of the essence of the Father, God of God], Light of Light,
very God of very God, begotten, not made, being of one
substance with the Father.

What a difference in language, content and delivery. How would
John the apostle and gospel writer have reacted to this? Even
though he understood Greek and basic philosophy, these words
would have brought him a deep sadness. *What has happened to*
our simple belief in Almighty God and His son, Jesus the Messiah
of mankind?

The Ten Commandments and the Sermon on the Mount were
expressions of Hebraic thought and were concerned with conduct,
how God's people ought to act. By contrast, the Nicene Creed
was mostly a result of Greek thought, concerned so much with
definitions and legalities, because so much that had been taken on
faith by the earliest Christians was now immersed in doubt thanks
to the wave of rationalism that had swept into the Church from
the Greek philosophers. As a result the simple faith of Jesus Christ
had taken backward steps, constantly having to redefine itself to a
sceptical public, unable to move forwards. You can imagine God's
heartfelt cry, *hey I'm here, I've always been here, how can we move*
on into a real relationship if you keep doubting me?

The reason why many Christians were now able to get away
with appalling conduct was because they considered correct belief
(as determined by "Christian philosophers") more important than
correct behaviour. Hence the persecutions, massacres, "holy wars"
and anti-semitism, followed by the bloody Crusades and the nasty
Inquisition that were the legacy of the Christian Middle Ages.

Christianity was starting to become a philosophical system,
fuelled by rational argument rather than the supernatural acts of
God. Greek rationalism had won over Hebraic faith.

Now we move forward, nine centuries after Nicea, and arrive
back at Thomas Aquinas, our Christian philosopher. He is writing
his master-work, his attempt at creating a systematic Christianity,

integrating Greek reason with Hebraic faith. His book is called the *Summa Theologica.*

The Summa starts with God, then considers man and his purpose, then explains the need for Christ and finishes with the sacraments. In building his arguments Thomas quotes from an exalted panel of historical experts, the vast majority of them non-Christian and familiar to us. There was Aristotle ("The Philosopher"), Averroes ("The Commentator"), Augustine ("The Theologian") and Maimonides ("Rabbi Moses"). Others include Dionysius (Greek), Ulpian (Roman) and Avicenna (Muslim). In other words, a most inclusive list of experts to create a book that was to become the most influential source book for Catholic doctrine for centuries to come.

But there's a twist to this. It appears that Thomas never finished the book; the *Summa Theologica* is an unfinished work. While writing the final section on the sacraments it was said that he had a mystical experience. When asked about it, he replied, "*all that I have written seems to me like so much straw compared to what I have seen and what has been revealed to me.*" He died three months later. It is fanciful to wonder about the nature of his experience. What had been revealed to him to cause him to make such a statement? Was he having second thoughts about his writings? It mattered little as he died soon later and the Church took this unfinished work and it became a hugely influential work of theology, right up to modern times.

A movement, *scholasticism*, flourished as a result of his teachings. It marked the beginning of the great European Universities and was a school system acting as a practical expression of Thomas's ideas, that of marrying together philosophy and theology. As a result of this, Aristotle was able to gain a strong foothold on the medieval mind.

Meanwhile there were even stronger influences on the medieval mind in the form of the popes, supposedly God's supreme representatives on Earth. What a sorry story there is to tell there, but here is not the place to give any more than a basic overview.

Suffice to say, most of the medieval popes were characterised by all the very worst that can be dragged from the darkest places of the human soul. Let's just consider one of these popes, Alexander VI, an active member of a prominent Italian crime family, the Borgias. Rising through the ranks, thanks to strings pulled by his uncle (also a pope), he acquired pope-dom allegedly through bribery. Once enthroned it became a family affair. His illegitimate son became Archbishop of Valencia at the age of 17. Another son became a duke and his daughter married a lord. He also gave away a lot of papal land to his children. Alexander himself was a party animal and his wild orgies within the papal palaces were widely reported (though denied now by the Catholic Church). He was also alleged to be a murderer.

God's representative on Earth, eh? Something had to give. By the 15th Century the whole structure of the Catholic Church from the top down was riddled with corruption. Greek thinking had triumphed in every possible way. The *dualism* of Platonism had ensured that the masses were kept at bay, separated from those in "holy" professions such as the popes and the clergy, as if by divine right. The *rationalism* of Aristotle continued to tie people up into knots, focussing on the cleverness of the scholars, rather than following the example of those truly living out the Christian life. And we haven't even started to cover the doctrines that defined the Catholic Church of the day, from the doctrine of transubstantiation to such ideas as purgatory, indulgences and praying for the dead.

Transubstantiation is the belief that, as part of the Eucharist, Holy Communion, the bread and wine *actually* change into the body and blood of Christ on the altar. This indeed is a strange one. Jesus Christ present, in person, rather than just being present *symbolically*? Aristotle taught that there is more to matter than its appearance. Every object also has *substance,* a kind of inner quality which defines it. An example given is that when water freezes it takes on a different appearance (ice), but is still the same substance (H_2O). Given this Greek understanding, Thomas Aquinas said that at the point of consecration at Holy Communion, although their appearance doesn't change, the *substance* of the bread and wine does, miraculously changing into the body and blood of Christ.

Purgatory, indulgences and praying for the dead are Catholic ideas that, although not overtly Greek in background, neither do they have authentic Biblical origin. This brings up the important point, touched upon in the previous chapter, of *tradition*, the habit of religious systems, including Rabbinic Judaism and Roman Catholicism, to place thoughts and ideas of men above or alongside divine revelation.

Purgatory was said to be a half-way house for souls, a temporary waiting room for those who have not quite earned their way to Heaven. Praying for the dead is a way to improve their chances for Heaven and indulgences – a sort of reward for good works – are a way of doing a deal with the Church to minimise one's own time in purgatory.

They were all part of the same package, a self-help fast-track to Heaven without the need of true repentance for one's own sins and faith in the sacrifice of Jesus Christ. Each of them benefited the Church financially or helped to maintain the status-quo in an uncertain age, or both. It was a shameful disgrace, a corruption of true faith and served to control the lives of the common man, by convincing them that only the Church could get you to Heaven. Individual responsibility was more or less unheard of; after all no-one even had access to Bibles in their own language, so the Church had full control over what was understood of God's Word. You couldn't blame ordinary people, but the Church had an awful lot to answer for!

Enough is enough, already! Surely, for the sake of the faithful remnant of believers, God had to do something, so He did. He stirred up the people who took Him seriously, rather than those who used the Church to live off immoral earnings. Many stood up to the plate and suffered the consequences. Although Martin Luther was the one credited with the breakthrough, many consider the Dutch priest, Erasmus, as the one who lit the fuse. He was one of the first early Christian humanists, a movement that shifted focus away from the Church institution and towards the needs of the individual. Erasmus sought for reformation *within* the Church, through education and social change. He even created a new translation of the New Testament into Greek, which was incredibly influential, not least with Luther himself.

The Reformation was mostly a good thing. But not in every way. The Catholic Church was ripe for some major reforms and the Protestant Reformation performed a sterling service, but they didn't go far enough for one commentator. Our man is Jacob (Yacov) Prasch, a gifted teacher on the Hebraic roots of Christianity, who has much to say about the Reformation. I will briefly explain his thoughts on the matter.

When the Reformers came along they were in a unique position. They had a chance to wipe the slate clean, clear out all of the dross and introduce the authentic gospel of Jesus Christ, based on the promise given in Jeremiah 31:31-34, the clearest announcement for the New Covenant in the Old Testament.

> *"The time is coming," declares the LORD, "when I will make a new covenant with the house of Israel and with the house of Judah. It will not be like the covenant I made with their forefathers when I took them by the hand to lead them out of Egypt, because they broke my covenant, though I was a husband to them," declares the LORD. "This is the covenant I will make with the house of Israel after that time," declares the LORD. "I will put my law in their minds and write it on their hearts. I will be their God, and they will be my people. No longer will a man teach his neighbor, or a man his brother, saying, 'Know the LORD,' because they will all know me, from the least of them to the greatest," declares the LORD. "For I will forgive their wickedness and will remember their sins no more."*

This New Covenant was not made with the "Church" but with Israel and the Jews. It is a Jewish covenant, with provisions made for Gentiles to be grafted into the "olive tree" (Romans 11). The

Catholics turned this on its head and made it a New Covenant for Gentiles, with the Jewish branches replaced. The reformers did nothing to change this and just added their own branches in. The Hebraic form and content of the New Covenant was ignored and the same old Greek tools were used to interpret it, including *allegory,* to spiritualise anything about Israel as being for the Church. Martin Luther made so much of the book of Romans, in his "discovery" of justification by faith, yet chose to ignore the plain meaning of the "Jewish" chapters 9 – 11.

As with the Catholics, many Reformers insisted that the curses of the Old Testament remain literally for Israel, while the blessings are spiritualised for the Church. If God is finished with the Jews, history shows us that the sins of the Church vastly outweigh anything the Jews got up to in Biblical times, so surely the Church is living off borrowed time! Fortunately for both Israel and the Church, the Covenants of God are not conditional on man's conduct, but rather on the unchanging promises of God.

What else did they get wrong? Just looking at the Anglican Church, there was far more continuation of Catholic ideas than surely would have been healthy for a process of reform. In the Book of Common Prayer, a baby is pronounced "Christian" simply through the sprinkling of water of "baptism", this being the condition of entry to the "Church of England". Justification by faith alone, anybody? And any member of the C of E automatically becomes a citizen of the British Commonwealth, a situation that Jacob calls a *regal papacy*! He continues, "Anglicanism is but one expression of the errors of the Reformers. Presbyterian, Lutheran, and Reform churches all have the same built-in error — a state church where people become members, not by new birth, but by being born into a state church and culture, and having an initiation ritual performed as babies."

Despite their battle-cry of *Sola Scriptura* ("Scripture alone"), the Reformers, as with the Catholics, relied rather too much on Augustine, and, by implication on Plato. By equating Christian identity with the *national* and cultural identity, as with the good ol'

C of E, this was an outworking of the replacement of Israel with the Church. The Church had become a nation within a nation, a Protestant Church State, an equivalent of the Nation of Israel, with structure and hierarchy, despite the whole purpose of the faith in Jesus Christ as being a collection of redeemed individuals united by a common purpose to evangelise the World.

The Reformation had not made the World a more peaceful place. In fact one of the bloodiest periods of history was the period after the Reformation when the Catholics and Protestants fought each other like blood-crazed bulldogs in a cage. Christians hated each other to the point of death, over matters of doctrine. In Catholic Spain great public executions were held where Protestants were burned to death, or disemboweled or decapitated. In England it was the other way round, but with the same end product.

It was the same old, same old...

Reasonable Doubt?

Thomas Aquinas and his followers had unleashed a genie from the lamp that was going to grow so large, so powerful, that one day it would attempt to engulf its master. The intentions may have been good to create a system whereby the rationalism of Aristotle could be harnessed as a servant to the understanding of the Word of God, but the outcome was eventually to prove fatal. A day was going to come when the critical faculties, the rational mind, even basic common sense, were going to look at the sorry state of the Church, whether Protestant or Catholic, and say, *what have we helped to create. Surely this couldn't have been what Jesus had in mind?!*

This indeed happened a few years earlier. It started with the Muslims with a massive military victory at Constantinople, the home of the "Christian Empire" that had stood for over a Millennium. History books declare this as the official end of the Middle Ages. Why would that be and what came next? Well, it was all largely a consequence of this very event, as refugees from Turkey arrived in Italy and helped to fuel a major new thing that was happening there, particularly in Florence: The Renaissance.

It was said to be the rebirth of classical culture after centuries of darkness and barbarism. This *rebirth* comes to us as a French word, *Renaissance*. (By rights it should have been the Italian word, but try getting your tongue around *Renascimento).*

Let's repeat that sentence. *The rebirth of classical culture after centuries of darkness and barbarism.* The implications here are sad and awesome. It states the truism that "Christian" Europe was a time of darkness and barbarism and mankind was only saved by restoring the "virtues" and mindset of Ancient Greece. Yet, as we now know, it was the corruption of the Christian gospel by the very mindset of Ancient Greece that largely created the darkness and barbarism in the first place. What a tangled web we weave...

The seeds of the Renaissance were sown a century earlier by an Italian scholar called Petrarch. An avid student of the "ancient texts", he was one of the first *humanists*, though, as that term wasn't invented until 1808, he wouldn't have recognised the title. *Humanism*, this is a new concept. We are now starting to see, in "Christian" Europe, the beginnings of a movement that would start to push God aside and put man at the centre of the Universe.

One of Petrarch's main influences, and hence one of the key influences of the Renaissance, was our old friend Augustine, who in turn of course was primarily influenced by Plato. Whereas Aristotle's influence was to turn people's minds to the World around them, Plato told people to look within, which Petrarch did and concluded that man had to look inside himself and there to find salvation. Hence humanism emphasised the *dignity of man.*

So the Renaissance, that flowering of artistic, scientific and intellectual endeavour, lit up by such as Leonardo da Vinci, Raphael and Michelangelo, was not a movement primarily to the glory of God (though much of the art was of a religious nature), but to the glory of man and his possibilities. This sea-change can be seen through the syllabi of the schools of the time, as compared to an earlier age. Whereas the schools of the Middle Ages would have offered Latin, letter-writing and philosophy to their students, supplementing their religious instructions, a Renaissance student would typically major on grammar, rhetoric, poetry, history and moral philosophy. Horizons were being widened, outside the claustrophobic clutches of the Church. The Renaissance thinkers still saw themselves as "Sons of Adam", still saw themselves as part of the divine order. God was not out of the picture... yet!

But His days were numbered. By the start of the 17th Century, philosophers were appearing on the scene, willing to think the unthinkable. They intended to carry through Renaissance thinking even further... and take God out of the equation. They set out to view the World away from the restrictions of religious dogma and more in the spirit of... you've guessed it... Ancient Greece.

One of the first was Rene Descartes, said to be the Father of Modern Philosophy. He was not a fan of Aristotle, whose philosophy was so entrenched in the thinking of the Church that some churchmen believed that anyone who went against his principles was holding an anti-God position and ought to be punished. And, of course, the Church was quite strong on punishing, so Descartes was quite a brave man, particularly as a Roman Catholic. He preferred to search within and, of course, we know him from the Latin phrase, cogito ergo sum, *I think therefore I am.*

Out of this statement came a whole philosophy, a form of *rationalism* which was thoroughly man-centred, with a resolve to doubt everything that could be doubted, God included. The starting point for this new thinking was the human "self", one's own existence, the only thing that couldn't be doubted. It was the birth of *individualism*, a way of looking at the World that is still with us, as the defining feature of modern society. Yet, as already stated, Descartes was a Catholic, so he also used his philosophy to prove God's existence.

Then came a group of British philosophers known as the *empiricists*. They believed that what was most important was experience, figuring out the World through what could be seen, heard and touched, rather than by working things out rationally. The first was John Locke, who believed that we are born with minds like blank slates, empty and ready to be filled in through the experiences of a lifetime. He still hung on to a belief in God, but he was followed by one who didn't, a Scot called David Hume. He was also a sceptic and spent an awful lot of his time disproving the existence of God, philosophically. A life wasted, from God's point of view. Another philosopher worthy of mention here was the German, Immanuel Kant, whose major contribution was to create a compromise between the empiricists and the rationalists.

These philosophers were at the beginning of a movement later termed the *Enlightenment*. Just consider these movements. First we had the Renaissance, the "new birth" and now we have the Enlightenment, the emerging into the light of a new dawn. It was as if history had been stood on its head and was running backwards. Out of a period of history ignited by the truth of the gospel, we end up entering a "Dark Age" of oppression, ignorance and hatred and consider it a relief that we emerge from this into the light. That's what the *gospel* was meant to do! The *new birth* and the *emerging from darkness into light* is the Christian "thing". It's not meant to be a rescue *from* the gospel. That's how low the Christian Church had sunk; it had departed so much from what it was meant to be, that mankind felt that it had to be rescued from it, using the very mindset, that of Plato in particular, that had doomed it in the first place!

At around the same time there were some philosophers who still held onto a belief in God... but only just! They were the *Deists*. They believed that God created everything – lit the fuse, so to speak – then shuffled off and left the World for humanity to do what it liked. God as absentee landlord, you could say.

It was a belief that made room for rationalism but which did away with all the important parts of Christianity, like faith in Jesus, prophecy and miracles. Two famous Deists were Rousseau and Voltaire as were, allegedly and controversially, many of the founding fathers of the USA.

This seems like a crutch, like safety wheels on a bike, an unwillingness to let go of the idea of God, though this is not the God as described in the Bible, as a living, loving, involved Divine Person, but rather a detached uninvolved figure with access to the "master switch". It seems that this view just needed a slight nudge for the whole house of cards to come tumbling down.

Meanwhile, in the 18th Century, all was not going well in the mainstream Church. The Church of England was becoming fat, inactive and ineffectual. A quick kick in the rump was what was needed and John Wesley duly obliged. What the *Methodists* showed was that, despite all the over-intellectualising and emphasis on doctrine and division that had infiltrated the Church through the influences of Plato (with the Protestants) and Aristotle (with the Catholics), God was still alive.

God was fed up with the dross and, using the sincere desire of Wesley and George Whitefield to reform the Church of England, brought about a sovereign unleashing of power and grace. This was true revival. While it lasted it brought great fruit externally and internally. Thousands were brought into New Birth, justified by true faith in Jesus Christ and the hallmarks of this movement were relentless preaching, bible study groups and manifestations of the Holy Spirit. There was nothing Greek about all of this, it was a throwback to the Hebraic spirit of the very First Church of the Book of Acts.

The Lord God had squeezed into history at a time when His very existence was being doubted like never before. The people needed reminding what it was all about, what the purpose of their existence was. There had been too much chitter-chatter; what was needed was a demonstration of His power.

It's a shame that the revival took a name, grew a structure, a hierarchy and became just another denomination, with annual budgets, an investment portfolio and a corporate website.

The 19th Century brought about a range of competing movements, some good, some bad, all depending on your viewpoint. Taking our viewpoint as a reference, here is the story of that century, starting with the good, then working downwards.

Let's be reminded of Jesus' Great Commission, the job of the Christian and the Church.

"Therefore go and make disciples of all nations, baptizing them in the name of the Father and of the Son and of the Holy Spirit,

*and teaching them to obey everything I have commanded you.
And surely I am with you always, to the very end of the age."*
(Matthew 28:19-20)

In all the centuries of the Church very little of this had been done,
except at the point of the sword, with the threat of *accept my
doctrines or die*, rather than making disciples through the exercise
of love. The 19th Century was going to change all this.

William Carey, a cobbler from Northamptonshire, became one of
the greatest missionaries since the days of the apostles. In 1792 he
wrote a pamphlet, "an Enquiry into the Obligation of Christians
to use Means for the Conversion of Heathen." It had an incredible
effect and the following year Carey effectively launched the modern
missionary movement. Within just a hundred years Bible translations
multiplied fivefold and mission organisations grew from seven to
about 100. Missionaries were sent out to every corner of the World,
converting tribes and discipling nations and within a century the
number of professing Christians had more than doubled.

There were the *Great Awakenings* in America. The first was
sparked off by George Whitefield from England, featuring the great
preacher and theologian, Jonathan Edwards. The second, featuring
Charles Finney, brought great social reforms and a great "back to
the roots" movement of a more authentic Christianity. The third,
lasting the whole second half of the century, brought a lot of
religious fervour, though not all of it on the positive side.

Out of this came a great feeling that God was either about to
wrap things up or provide new revelations to His Church, or both.
A lot of strange ideas came creeping out of the woodwork and the
interesting thing to note is how many of them were simple re-hashes
of ancient heresies, inspired by the teachings of Plato.

The Jehovah's Witnesses' central deviation from normal
Christian belief is that they believe that Jesus is a created being,
less than fully divine. This is just *Arianism* from the 4th Century,
a consequence of the dualism of Plato that could not conceive of a
spiritual God actually having a physical body.

The Mormons may have smiling faces, homespun wisdom and sharp suits, but underneath it all is not just dodgy underwear, but some very strange beliefs. If we start with *Arianism* (relegating Jesus to a created being) and work our way through to *Gnosticism* (claiming special revelation), then you get an idea where they are coming from.

Theosophy is another cult harking back to Plato, as well as Eastern mysticism. Spiritism claims both Plato and Socrates as precursors to Christ. One doesn't even know where to start with Christian Science, neither "Christian" nor "Science", with enough deviations from mainstream Christian belief to keep Justin Martyr and Tertullian occupied for a whole lifetime. A heresy of heresies!

What were the Catholics up to in the 19th Century? They were regrouping. They found a champion in John Henry Newman, a convert from the Church of England and, at the time of writing, on the shortlist for imminent sainthood. He became a highly influential Catholic apologist. Here's a quote from him that is quite telling. He is speaking of the Church Fathers:

> *They do not speak of their own private opinion; they do not say, "This is true, because we see it in Scripture"—about which there might be differences of judgment—but, "this is true, because in matter of fact it is held, and has ever been held, by all the Churches, down to our times, without interruption, ever since the Apostles."*

(The Patristical Idea of Antichrist: Lecture 1)

He is stating that interpretation of Scripture is the responsibility of the Church, as handed down. In other words he has reinforced the idea that the Church Fathers never used Holy Scripture as proof-texts, but rather to back up Church tradition. The Catholics emphasise tradition, from the Church Fathers onwards, as the touchstone of their understandings of Scripture, rather than the Scripture itself.

Tradition! It's that word again. If the Reformers got one thing right, it was *Sola Scriptura*, Scripture alone. This has to be our bedrock. If we relied rather on the shifting sands of human wisdom, particularly human beings heavily influenced by pagan philosophy, then we're well and truly sunk. God has made it so easy for us. He put the whole thing in one book. He says to us, *there it all is, everything you need to find salvation and meaning and live your lives in a Godly way.* Just a single book, small enough to fit in your pocket.

The Bible has a single author, God. We know Him, we can trust Him – if we can't then the issue is with us, not Him. With tradition we are putting our trust in a whole shipload of fallible men, none of whom we've met.

Here's an example. The doctrine of the *Immaculate Conception* is a doctrine announced by the pope in 1854 as a Catholic truth. In a nutshell, this states that Mary, the mother of Jesus, was conceived without original sin.

Here is how Cardinal Newman defends the doctrine. Firstly he appeals to tradition, the writings of the Church Fathers, in order to find a connection between Mary, the mother of Jesus and Eve, the mother of mankind. Now, we know Jesus is the "Second (or last) Adam", because Scripture tells us:

> So it is written: "The first man Adam became a living being"; the last Adam, a life-giving spirit.
> (1 Corinthians 15:45)

Newman declares Mary to be the "Second Eve", with the Second Eve being mother to the Second Adam! This huge jump in logic is defended by reference to the all-too-fallible Church Fathers, Justin Martyr, Tertullian, Cyril and Irenaeus.

He then looks at Eve and suggests that (before the Fall) she was endowed with a super-abundance of grace, as if it is a measurable physical attribute. If so, then why couldn't Mary have been born with the same advantages? All conjecture, all assumptions, all guesswork!

He then tackles a loophole in the Scripture that speaks plainly against his position:

But now a righteousness from God, apart from law, has been made known, to which the Law and the Prophets testify. This righteousness from God comes through faith in Jesus Christ to all who believe. There is no difference, for all have sinned and fall short of the glory of God, and are justified freely by his grace through the redemption that came by Christ Jesus.
(Romans 3:21-26)

Newman looks for conditions and exceptions in something that looks clear-cut. Rather than accepting that *all* have sinned, meaning everyone – including Mary – he says that, as there is an obvious exception to this in Jesus himself, then *why couldn't Mary be an exception too*, particularly as she is the *second* Eve, with this *super-abundance of grace*.

So from this human reasoning he believes that Mary never sinned, because, unlike the rest of humankind, she was not stained by original sin. This whole process that Newman went through is called *eisegesis*, reading something into Scripture that wasn't there to start with, just to support your position, rather than *exegesis*, gaining an understanding from what is already in Scripture.

Now back to the *Deists*. These folk, who had relegated God to the role as *the one who got the Universe started*, were still around in the 19th Century. It was a popular position for some in the upper-classes who were – let us say – somewhat brain-challenged. *God is an Englishman* they would cry, while turning a blind eye at the crippling poverty, child exploitation and other evils afflicting the not-so-well-off in Victorian England. Authentic Christianity for the chattering classes was fighting on all fronts – science, philosophy, history – and generally losing. Science, fuelled by Greek rationalism, was opening folk's minds to new possibilities and, as these minds were tuning away from the supernatural and towards the rational, it only needed one small nudge... which came courtesy of Charles Darwin, who was the one who made the necessary discoveries.

The concept of evolution was around long before Darwin. He was just the one who went looking for the evidence to support it. The first to propose the idea of common ancestors was yet another Ancient Greek, Anaximander, in the 6th Century BC. In Darwin's day, his own grandfather, Erasmus, had spoken much about evolution, and had even written a poem about it. The atheists and rationalists just needed someone to furnish the facts that would dress the theory of evolution and allow her to parade herself in public in all her finery. Because, if one didn't even need a God to get *Life, the Universe and everything* started, there was no need even to be a Deist, let alone a proper Christian! Mankind could be free at last from "divine tyranny"! In other words, evolution was an idea waiting for a methodology long before Charles Darwin appeared. A thoroughly Greek worldview required a saviour and Darwin duly obliged.

But the really bad stuff in the 19th Century was happening in Germany and I'm not even going to cover the anti-Semitic and racial theories developed there, that were eventually going to lead to the rise of Nazism and the Holocaust. I'm not even going to mention the dark, soulless deliberations of Karl Marx and Frederick Nietzsche. Instead we focus on a direct attack on the Word of God, the Bible, itself... by Christians!

One attack was on the Old Testament, led by Julius Wellhausen, a German professor of the... Old Testament! He took the five books of the Torah and using the full tools of Greek logic and understanding, completed the job first started by Philo nearly 2000 years earlier. He analysed the Holy Scripture from all angles – historical, social, literary – bar one – the evidence of a supernatural authorship – and sucked away all evidence of the Holy Spirit's work. He produced something called the *documentary hypothesis*, an attack on Moses as the author of the Torah, still with us today, courtesy of liberal Christians of all persuasions.

Another attack was on the New Testament. Another German, Hermann Reimarus, a Deist, was one of many who entered a quest for the *historical Jesus*, a Jesus with all "mythology" swept away, an anaemic Jesus who travelled around the Holy Land doing nice things and saying nice things. A Jesus of revisionist history, but not the Jesus of the Bible, the miracle-working prophet who died for our sins and who was miraculously resurrected.

There we leave the broad sweep of the 19th Century, a time of great change, of many new beginnings, and of ideas and movements that form the tapestry of life today in the 21st Century.

To Cut a Long Story Short

So here's where we are so far. A short summary; a reward for those of you who persevered with the last four chapters and a refuge for those of you who didn't.

The Church first hit the rails as soon as the original apostles had died, leaving the legacy of Jesus in the hands of Gentiles educated in the Greek-speaking world and immersed in the philosophic ideas of Ancient Greece, particularly Plato. Heresies, such as *Marcionism* and *Gnosticism*, abounded, born out of corruptions of God's word through the ideas from Greek philosophy and these were countered through the efforts of early Church fathers such as Justin Martyr and Ireneaus, who, themselves were self-styled Christian philosophers. So the Christian world in those days was fought over by Greeks versus Greeks, with the only real casualty being the gospel itself.

It was in the ancient city of Alexandria when things really started to get worse, thanks firstly to the Church Father, Clement, who was by today's standard a heretic in all but name, and Origen, who did immeasurable damage in the area of Bible interpretation, popularising the use of *allegory* in his approach to Holy Scripture and opening up the floodgates for ages to come, allowing "teachers" to coax any meaning they liked out of their reading of the Bible.

Then came the Dark Ages, a period of ignorance, superstition and... darkness. Although the Bible was now available, few could actually read it, apart from the professional class of Christians, the *clergy*. Some of the blame for these sorry times could be laid at the feet of the foremost Christian teacher of that day, Augustine. He wrote a book, *City of God*, as a defence of Christianity against the paganism that surrounded it. In the book, he encouraged his readers, in a Christian take on the dualism of Platonism, to pay less attention to their lives and, instead, look heavenwards at the "city yet to come", the *City of God*, or Heaven. Hence the Dark Ages, when nobody really cared about anything apart from the promises of the after-life, which were dictated by the State Church with its system of sacraments, rather than by the authentic route of repentance of sins and trust in the death and resurrection of Jesus Christ!

In the 8th Century the works of another Greek philosopher, Aristotle, were discovered by the Muslims and translated by the Jews into the languages of the day. By introducing the concept of *rationalism* into the religious cultures of the Jews, Muslims and Christians, it is fair to say that the damage done was immense. These ideas were taken up by the most influential Christian philosopher of the Middle Ages, Thomas Aquinas, who created a religious system combining faith and reason, stating that even the existence of God was not to be taken as a given but through analysis of information that could be gathered by the senses.

The genie had been let out and the subsequent rise of rationalism was to eat away at the certainties of faith. State Christianity became more of a philosophic system to be argued over rather than a supernatural expression of God's plans for mankind. This was not helped by the corruptions of the Catholic Church and its use of pagan practices to control the ordinary people. Something had to give and it was Martin Luther who provided the spark of a *Reformation* in the Church, a new beginning.

Yet even the Reformers were not free from Greek influences, following the Platonism of Augustine in many of their ideas, as distinct from the Roman Catholics, who stuck to the Aristotleism of Thomas Aquinas. It was the accent on the rationalism of Aristotle that was to spearhead the next major attack on the Christian Church, which has lasted from the end of the Middle Ages right up until today. First came the *Renaissance*, the "rebirth", the flowering of culture and artistic expression in Italy, believe it or not inspired by the ideals of Ancient Greece! This was also the birth of *Humanism,* a movement that placed man at the centre of everything, rather than God. Then came the philosophers of the *Enlightenment*, who built on these ideas and eventually totally did away with the need for God at all, replacing Him with their own rational ideas. This was the birth of *Individualism*, which has now become the defining feature of modern society.

Although God made something of a comeback thanks to the Methodist movement, followed by the awakenings of the 18th and 19th Centuries, prompting a massive worldwide missionary movement, we largely entered an age of confusion and division. This was the age of new cults, such as Christian Science and the Jehovah's Witnesses, born out of the ancient Greek heresies. It was also an age of a fight back by the Catholics, with strange new doctrines such as the *immaculate conception*. There were the Deists, who believed in some kind of absentee landlord God and then there was Charles Darwin and his ideas, to further chip away at the ancient faith, with the mallet of human reason and scientific methodology. And out of Germany came *Higher Criticism*, a new way to disbelieve the Bible.

Which brings us to the modern age, where our story continues...

A Fine Mess ...

Does this ring a bell? You meet someone at a Church meeting. He's a Christian and he makes an immediate impression on you. But not a good impression. Through the course of a single conversation, he strikes you as proud, judgemental, a little arrogant and very sure of his strongly held beliefs and dismissive of others. He's dressed smartly, his Bible is in a smart leather wallet and in that short time you have been fed a whole catalogue of his dislikes, from women ministers to liberals.

A word comes to mind, it's a word we tend to use for those who are entrenched in traditionalism, are legalistic in nature and take great store from outward appearances. We call them *Pharisees*.

We could go further and conduct a little survey of others around us at that meeting. There's a lady in the corner with a haughty expression. She has been with the church her whole life, since she was sprinkled as a baby. She serves on the Parish Council and believes totally in this church and the great work it does in the community. Trouble is that she believes in little else, certainly not in the great revealed truths and miracles of the Bible, such as the Resurrection, Heaven and Hell. Scientific rationalism and "human progress" have done for whatever little faith she had. If she had been around in Jesus' day, she would have been identified mostly with the *Sadducees*.

You continue with your exercise. You find quite a few *Zealots*, Christians not averse to a bit of political action. There's even an *Essene*, a puzzled young man in the corner, keeping his own counsel who, when pressed, had some very strange ideas and was not over-keen to share them. Of course there are also representatives of that 1st Century Jewish sect called *The Way*, disciples of Jesus and now calling themselves Christians. In fact everyone you meet in that church claims to be in that group, but only some will tick all the boxes.

> *"Enter through the narrow gate. For wide is the gate and broad is the road that leads to destruction, and many enter through it. But small is the gate and narrow the road that leads to life, and only a few find it."*
> (Matthew 7:13-14)

It's an interesting exercise to see the connections over a 2000 year gap but it's not a realistic exercise, because a lot has happened in that 2000 years and most of it is not very good. Can we honestly say that we are closer to God and His purposes than those first disciples, following *The Way* of Jesus? And if so, then we have to concede that the 2000 year journey has been a bumpy ride of many distractions. We wonder at the misfortunes of the Children of Israel, doomed to 40 year wanderings before entering the Promised Land. Now multiply that by a factor of around 25 and you get to see the fate of the Christian Church.

Of course it hasn't all been bad and many souls have lived and died and will live again in the presence of God. But not as many as there could have been.

> *"Not everyone who says to me, 'Lord, Lord,' will enter the kingdom of heaven, but only he who does the will of my Father who is in heaven."*
> (Matthew 7:21)

History is important, which is why the last few chapters may have seemed a chore, but were necessary to set a context, a framework for us to be able to look back and see where the Church went off the rails. Unlike Adam our Christian faith didn't just arrive on the scene fully formed, though many believe it has. What we sign up for depends on so many factors; matters of geography, culture, education, family background and social standing. Because we are not 1st Century Jews speaking Hebrew and Aramaic, with knowledge of the Hebrew Scriptures and Hebrew idioms, word play and even Jewish history, then we are all going to receive our faith with *extra toppings*. Where you live, how you are impacted by popular culture, your level of schooling, ethnic background, degree of family pressures and your material wealth, *they all matter*.

The apostles Paul and Peter had to make adjustments to cater for the non-Jews of their day; how much more do we need to do so today? History has shown us how Christianity has absorbed so much from the World, particularly philosophies from ancient Greece, at every level of its development. The result of this, as well as from the numerous other outside influences, is not just a plethora of denominations but, increasingly so these days, a huge spectrum of Christian worldviews.

How did the Lord find you? Have you been brought up in a Christian family and have always known Him? In which case, what denomination or grouping do your family come from – Baptist, Anglican, Pentecostal, charismatic, liberal, messianic or another? Of course you may have plotted your own course in life, in which case you could have spectacles tinted (or tainted) with all shades of politics, lifestyles, philosophies or religions.

You get my point? One truth, many routes, many dead ends and diversions. The problem is knowing whether you are on a route to the truth, or are being diverted away from it, or are on a one-way trip to nowhere. In this respect the Christian faith was dead easy for the first believers in Jesus – they just believed in him and followed the teachings of the first apostles, though even then there were signs of things to come.

I appeal to you, brothers, in the name of our Lord Jesus Christ, that all of you agree with one another so that there may be no divisions among you and that you may be perfectly united in mind and thought. My brothers, some from Chloe's household have informed me that there are quarrels among you. What I mean is this: One of you says, "I follow Paul"; another, "I follow Apollos"; another, "I follow Cephas"; still another, "I follow Christ."

(1 Corinthians 1:10-12)

Then as the faith spread geographically and other influences seeped in, there began to be many expressions of the Christian faith, resulting today in over 38,000 Christian denominations and groupings. One truth, 38,000 routes, but which to follow?

Rather than give you the full listing of the 38,000, with a report card and heresy index for each, we can get an appreciation of the problem by looking just at two expressions of Christianity, each spawning many groups and fellowships and each straddling a whole bunch of denominations.

The first is the *Word of Faith* movement. This is what you get when you scratch the surface of the prosperity teachers, with their impeccable dress sense, lavish lifestyles and perfect teeth. The secular world is appalled and amused by these people, but many Christians follow their exploits on TV, and a lot of them commit their finances to these ministries too, so it is a significant movement.

This is not an exposé or an attempt to ridicule these people; you only need to view the usual suspects on Youtube and they condemn themselves, if they are to be judged by Biblical standards. Instead it is worth examining the roots of what they uniquely believe.

When dealing with a big subject like this, it is best to zero in on core concepts, then keep digging and analysing and pray that God will shine some light on it, so that what is true and what is false are exposed. The best place to start here is the very title of the movement, the *Word of Faith* movement.

In a nutshell these teachers look at the two Greek words translated as "word" in the New Testament, that is *logos* and *rhema*. The simplest distinction between them is that logos refers to the "written" word and rhema the "spoken" word. These teachers have the understanding that, whereas logos should be used in the sense of reading the "word of God" as Holy Scripture, a *rhema* word is when a "word" of revelation is given to an individual believer, either through direct reading of the Bible, or from another person, such as a preacher from the platform/pulpit.

Although it is not for me to condemn or belittle this practice, what should concern us is the potential for its use in the manipulation of vulnerable people. When someone gives a *rhema* word out from the platform, a *thus says the Lord,* or *the Lord is doing a new thing* or *here's what you must do to get blessed,* one must ask the question, *why should God use these people in such a way? Can't He communicate with believers directly?* This is especially the case when this *rhema* word is either given as a "new revelation" or is just plain suspicious or wacky!

The other aspect to this teaching, also harking back to the title, is the invoking of "faith" as a key ingredient. If someone has sufficient "faith" for something, whether it is for a new car or a healing from illness, then the confessing of this need, they say, should be sufficient to receive it. This is also known as *name it and claim it!*

There are two warning beacons for this whole circus. Firstly, sensible historians and analysts have traced the *Word of Faith* movement to such 19th Century heresies as Christian Science, itself an aberration birthed in the teachings of Plato. So there's a definite Greek aroma about the whole thing. Secondly, and probably most relevantly, we have the recurring scenario of clergy vs laity, or in this case, the *special spiritual ones on the platform with supposed special knowledge* and those in the audience (sorry, congregation), who, although referred to as angels or partners, are usually just seen as convenient sources of cash to prop up the ministry. This is that old early Christian heresy, *Gnosticism,* pure and simple, best illustrated, as already described, by the story of Simon Magus, eager to exercise spiritual powers for spiritual gain.

It's ironic, particularly in the current recession that the faith and prosperity teachers seem to have little of either and watching them flounder on Christian TV is quite a spectator sport – finding new ways to prophetically fleece the flock!

At the other end of the Christian landscape are those modern-day inheritors of the "re-examinations" of Jesus and the Bible in the 19th Century. There is a general term for these folk, *liberals*, as in "liberated from the revealed truth of the Word of God and all that it implies".

I remember in my pre-Christian days chuckling at the burning of York Minster, the cathedral in the north of England. No, this was not born out of my negativity towards God, but, in fact, the opposite. Now I realise that it was one of the stepping stones that eventually led me to the feet of Jesus Christ. On July 9th 1984 the church was hit by lightning and the resultant blaze did enormous damage. This fact hit the headlines of the daily press in the UK because of one intriguing detail – just three days earlier David Jenkins had been consecrated in that very place as Bishop of Durham. And David Jenkins was the highest profile Anglican who was not afraid to admit that he did not believe in the virgin birth nor the physical resurrection of Jesus Christ. You can imagine the newspaper headlines; the press had a field day! *The conflagration and the consecration* boomed The Times. The tabloids were a little more succinct.

Way to go! cried I at the time, on a search for the truth and mightily impressed at the idea of God – in this day and age – showing His displeasure. *This is the kind of God I like!* The shock I felt at the time that the Church of England dismissed the whole episode as a coincidence and that *God doesn't do this sort of thing any more*, is still with me. The Bishop of Durham stayed in the job for ten years, during which time he was one of the first to bless a gay civil partnership and managed to get himself banned from preaching in some churches, for swearing in a sermon. What a glowing witness!

Now I realise that that *Doubting Durham* was simply representing a form of Christianity that I wrote about in the previous chapter, those Christian rationalists who were happy to relegate God to some vague role at Creation. They may call themselves liberals, as if this is a label to be proud of, but in fact they are just modern-day *Deists*, inheritors of the Aristotelian tradition.

Most modern liberal Christians, whether they know it or not, follow the ideas of a German theologian, who lived at the start of the 20th Century. Adolph Harnack was canny enough to discern that Christian doctrine was thoroughly infected by Greek thought. His solution was to throw out the lot and concentrate on three selected aspects of Jesus' teaching. He stressed the Fatherhood of God, the Brotherhood of Man and the value of the human soul. He desired to strip out the supernatural elements of Christianity, but emphasised what has become known as the "social gospel". It was man's reason put ahead of divine revelation. It was fed by new "advances" in science, particularly the theory of evolution that was now being used to prise God's fingers away from the only place the Deists found room for Him – the Creation.

Liberal Christianity now has a firm foothold in the modern Christian mind, thanks to the rise of rationalism, the new religion in our secular humanist society. Scientific apologists, helped by our secularised educational system, make their views so attractive so … reasonable and it is a tragedy in today's Church that so many have just rolled over without a fight and allowed Aristotle to claim victory.

There must be another way. Yes, there is. Can true Biblical Christianity fight back? In the words of a very famous modern statesman, "yes, we can!"

The fight back begins in the next part of our journey, but it's going to be messy! It is time for God to speak through His Word.

PART THREE

BATTLEGROUNDS

Where we review each of our battlegrounds in the light of Church history. We examine what Christians have said about the issues of Creation, Israel, salvation in Jesus alone, Hell and End Times and why they thought as they did.

The Real Battle

Cast your mind back to the story of Theodore Dusty in my prologue. If you've googled him you'll realise that he's just a figment of my imagination, a flesh-and-blood illustration. But truth can be stranger than fiction if you've followed the stories in recent years of Heaven's Gate, Waco, Jonestown or Charles Manson. A dysfunctional Christian upbringing plus egomania plus a Bible can be a very dangerous mix indeed. Each of these examples ended in tragedy for the innocent followers of a dangerous teacher, brought about by his very personal interpretation of Holy Scripture. But what of Theodore himself?

Yes, he was extremely Bible literate, brought up in a strict brethren environment and force-fed the Word of God, albeit in a very stifling, claustrophobic atmosphere. He took refuge in his teenage years through the calming pastime of fishing, where he befriended Andrej, an illegal Polish immigrant, also a Christian, who introduced him to the quirky world of numerology. To cut a long story short, Theodore's experiences, knowledge and growing messianic impulses combined to create a unique theology where he was the modern Noah, surrounded by folk from the immigrant community, known collectively as *The Fish People*. He was guided, characteristically, by a *new revelation* from God, which directed him to all the Bible verses he needed to validate his mission to save mankind. His core motivation was 2 Chronicles 2:17:

Solomon took a census of all the aliens who were in Israel, after the census his father David had taken; and they were found to be 153,600.

To Theodore it was the aliens, the immigrant community, who were to build not the Temple, as the context insists, but a new ark, to rescue the chosen few from God's fresh flood. Theodore's excitement was that through his calculations, the time had come, through the alignment of two other *key* verses:

Simon Peter climbed aboard and dragged the net ashore. It was full of large fish, 153, but even with so many the net was not torn.
(John 21:11)

Noah was six hundred years old when the floodwaters came on the earth.
(Genesis 7:6)

Firstly he connected all three verses *numerologically*, through the numbers 153,600 and 153 and 600. Secondly the *alignment* was brought about by the fact that Theodore had just reached his 600th birthday (calculated by further Scripture twisting) and that, with the birth of the Polish baby mentioned earlier, there were now exactly 153 Fish People in the community. The time had come, the flood was coming and his trip to the weather station "confirmed" it. So off they went to the ark they had built in the woods...

Yes, an extreme example, but there are countless Theodores out there, equally dangerous, but in less obvious ways. They, unfortunately, get all the validation for their strange ideas through the pages of the Bible. So, how come? We need to look closer at this Book of books.

The Bible may be considered a divine encyclopaedia but it is not ordered like one. Topics don't fall into neat indexed sections, but are threaded through the text in a myriad of literary styles. Thousands of years before the invention of hypertext and web links, the Bible was already structured like our modern day Internet, a seemingly infinite cloud of connections and pathways logically ordered not by the mind of the web page designer, but by the awesome mind of our resourceful God.

He provided a key to its understanding, a key that has unfortunately been lost to us. That key, ironically, was the human mind itself, a mind dedicated to a lifetime of study of and reverence for the written Word of God, a mind unpolluted by alien philosophy and pagan interpretations. Jesus and his contemporaries possessed that mind, but as history progressed and Biblical truth was invaded by the ideas of competing cultures, such as Greece and Rome, the ability was severely hampered.

A mind thoroughly familiar with the nuances of the Hebrew Scriptures is able to make the connections and feed the understanding of God's ways and plans for us. This is why Jesus was able to connect with the Jews of his time and so antagonise the religious leadership. They could see in his life and actions fulfilments or allusions to Scriptures from the Old Testament and acted on this knowledge accordingly, either in a positive way or a negative way.

We do not possess this mind, this Hebrew mindset, so, like baby chicks in the nest, we look up to the sky in hunger and anticipation waiting for enlightenment or, trustingly, we rely on the knowledge of others. But there are things we can do for ourselves first.

The following section may be familiar to you if you have read my last book ("How the Church lost The Way..."), as I have unashamedly lifted some of it from my chapter on the Jewish way of reading the Bible. I make no apologies for this, as the following information is crucial for your understanding at this point and there's no point re-inventing the wheel!

How do we read and interpret the Bible? How can we tell what is in the heart of God as we read His words? We begin with two

Greek words, *exegesis* and *eisegesis*. Exegesis is the act of reading the words of the Bible and receiving the truth that God put there. Eisegesis is the act of reading the words of the Bible and only receiving what agrees with your own ideas, as we saw with our friend Theodore Dusty. The first technique is, I hope you agree, the way we should approach the Bible.

Surely we all want to read the words of the Bible and receive the truth that God put there. So where do we start? Let's start in the Bible itself.

> *For Ezra had devoted himself to the study and observance of the Law of the LORD, and to teaching its decrees and laws in Israel.*
> (Ezra 7:10)

Ezra took seriously the study of the written word of God. The Hebrew word used here, translated as "study and observance" is *darash*. Ezra was the spiritual leader who led the Jews from exile in Babylon to Jerusalem and got them all reading their Scriptures! From this period in history we can trace the beginnings of synagogues, where Scriptures are read out and expounded on.

So our starting point must be with these Jews who were first blessed with the Word of God. We would do well, at this point, to remember what Paul said of the Jewish people.

> *Theirs is the adoption as sons; theirs the divine glory, the covenants, the receiving of the law, the temple worship and the promises. Theirs are the patriarchs, and from them is traced the human ancestry of Christ, who is God over all, forever praised! Amen.*
> (Romans 9:4-5)

The Bible that Jesus knew was written by Hebrews, for Hebrews and about Hebrews, in the Hebrew and Aramaic languages, using Hebrew idioms, poetic styles and writing styles. So a good place to start when trying to understand the Bible is to turn to the Jewish Jesus himself.

So far we have not strayed too far from the orthodox teaching of the Protestant Reformers on how to understand the Bible. It is called the *Grammatical Historic method* and all it means is that we put ourselves in the role of someone who would have heard the words in the original setting and how they would have understood the words in context. So, all we need to do is pretend we are a 1st Century Jew with an understanding of 1st Century Jewish matters. Not easy is it? No, but we can at least make an effort!

There are rules used by Jewish scholars in reading and understanding Scripture. These have been developed over a period of time by groups of scholars who, at the same time, were creating huge commentaries on the Bible, compiled into such volumes as the Talmud. As interesting as this is, it doesn't help us, as we are looking for tools that the modern Western mind can understand and use, not dreary old reference books to leaf through. We have enough of those in the Christian world!

Unfortunately we start off at a disadvantage. Jesus and his contemporaries, in common with Jews before him and after him, would have had an encyclopaedic knowledge of the Hebrew Scriptures, the Old Testament. Jewish boys would study the Torah (the first five books of the Bible) at the age of five, the oral "Traditions" at the age of ten and be trained in *halachot*, rabbinic legal decisions, at the ripe old age of 15! Scripture would be memorised because they didn't have laptops in those days, or even ready access to writing materials. They knew God's word like some of us know The Simpsons, past storylines of our favourite soaps, or the traits and foibles of the latest movie star. Many of us struggle to come up with just the basic facts of standard Bible stories, particularly if we weren't carted off to Sunday school when children. We just don't, by and large, have an instinctive grasp of the Hebrew Scriptures and, consequently, we are handicapped when it comes to using traditional Jewish tools for understanding God's Word.

But there is hope for us. They may have had the Biblical training from a young age, but we have computers and these electronic companions can simulate a whole lifetime of study and experience. It's both sad and handy, but we must look on the bright side and use whatever tools we have at our disposal!

Jesus did a lot of stuff. Virtually everything he did was to fulfil the words of prophets of an earlier age. He healed, he taught, he comforted, he corrected, he put people right with God. In doing so he was able to point to his actions as fulfilments to the writings of Isaiah, Jeremiah, the Psalms and many other places. He was able to do so because there was a general agreement among the Jews of his day as to what these Scriptures were saying. They knew how to make sense of their Scriptures. The question of interpretation was not an issue as they all shared the same tools for reading these sacred words. Not so today. Over the last 2000 years of Christianity we have developed so many ways of reading and interpreting the Bible, it seems that we can make Scriptures say whatever we want them to say, without any regard to what they are actually saying. As a result, unscrupulous men have got rich, dastardly acts have been committed and communities have been led astray. All because "the Bible says ...."

It seems to me that when confusion and uncertainty reigns, then going back to origins is no bad thing. As Christians, who do we take as the ultimate authority? Jesus, of course. Then surely, in terms of the Scriptures available to him in his day (the Old Testament), we must read them through the eyes of Jesus, a 1st Century Jew. To do this we don't necessarily need a knowledge of Hebrew and Aramaic, the written languages of Scripture in those days. What we do need is to get inside their heads and follow the thought processes that drove their understanding.

It would help if, say among the Dead Sea Scrolls, someone found a set of parchments under the heading of "Reading Scripture the Jesus way" or "Bible interpretation for the non-Hebrew mind". We are not given this luxury but we can piece together a good picture from fragments of information from various sources, either from that time itself or from later writings. So where do we start?

There's a buzzword in the world of Jewish Bible interpretation. It's a Hebrew word, *pardes*, meaning "orchard". It's an acronym, but a dangerous one, as it derives from medieval Jewish mysticism, but we can still use it now that we have the knowledge of its origins. It's an acronym of four Jewish methods of Bible interpretation – **p**'shat, **r**emez, **d**'rash and **s**od. It's the final component, *sod*, that provides the mystical element, delving into the area of secret meanings and numerical codes. Some of this is probably quite harmless and possibly even faith-building, but no-one is going to accuse me of leading folk astray, so out come the shears and, like any good gardener, my orchard has been well and truly pruned! Out goes the sod.

This leaves us with three methods of Biblical interpretation and we shall look at each in turn.

First we have *p'shat*, a word that means "simple rendering" and encourages us to first take the plain simple meaning of the Scripture you are reading. This is easy, no computers needed here. In fact this method is basically the same as the traditional Christian method mentioned earlier, the *Grammatical Historic method.* In this you take the literal meaning of the text – the plain sense of what you are reading – with attention given to the grammar (the form of the words), the context (looking at the other verses before and after this one) and the historical meaning (who is talking, who is he talking to, where they are talking, and when they were talking).

This is reading the Bible in the same way as we read anything, from a trashy novel to a motorcycle maintenance manual. We take the plain sense of what we are reading. When Lady Alice decides to take her butler Geoffrey on a cruise of the South Seas, we assume they are booking tickets on a liner rather than sharing some metaphysical vision. When you are warned against the engine oil of your motorbike falling below the minimum level, we are talking about a straight forward physical measurement, rather than an issue of the quality of the oil or making an allegorical statement about your moral standing. When God makes promises to Abraham about his descendants and where they will live, we can assume that is exactly what He is talking about, in its literal sense. That's how Jesus would have seen it.

The second method is *remez*, meaning "to hint". This goes a bit deeper and takes us into the areas of typology (where something in the Old Testament connects with something later on in the New Testament), symbolism (where something in the Old Testament represents something else) and allegory (which you have already met). Beware murky waters, because sharks and other predators lurk within, seeking to devour you. Because once we veer away from the safety of *p'shat* and its literal meaning we can fall prey to those who claim special understandings. This is a minefield, not only because of the charlatans of the Christian world but because of certain interpretations of Scripture that have been passed down from generation to generation, using the mind-set and tools developed by our Greek philosophers and their Christian devotees.

Another form of remez would be going a little deeper and using the technique we have already heard about, *allegory*. We have seen these techniques when we looked at Origen and Augustine and how they derived their allegorical methods from the teachings of Plato. So is all allegory bad? There's a real danger of *throwing out the baby with the bath water*, as there is good allegory and bad allegory. Good allegory has been put there by God to give us a deeper truth and a bad allegory is the product of a human mind that either rejects the literal reading of the text and/or feels that they have a "special revelation" to interpret the text in a certain way.

Here is a good allegory: Jesus is referred to as the Lamb of God, or refers to himself as the Good Shepherd. These can be backed up by Old Testament Scriptures, from Isaiah and Ezekiel, and connections can be made.

He was oppressed and afflicted, yet he did not open his mouth; he was led like a lamb to the slaughter, and as a sheep before her shearers is silent, so he did not open his mouth.
(Isaiah 53:7)

*My servant David will be king over them, and they will all have
one shepherd. They will follow my laws and be careful to keep
my decrees.*
(Ezekiel 37:24)

Then there is *bad* allegory... and we stumble into a minefield. Of
course, this is just my opinion and I will now state categorically
that I'm a *p'shat man*. I believe that, in common with Jesus and the
1st Century Jewish Christians, the Bible is to be understood, in the
first instance, in its literal sense, as *p'shat*. For those who disagree,
the only refuge is allegory. Either you believe in the clear narrative
of certain Bible passages, or you don't believe them and spiritualise
them as allegory.

Now that you've had some grounding, it is time to move to the
next step. We are now going to approach our five battlegrounds
mentioned way back in the introduction, five areas of conflict and
controversy. These areas are sidelined or ignored by most Christians
these days, because of the baggage that has become attached to
them. But the reality is that there is a real cost involved in taking a
position on these areas, because Biblical truth has been so obscured
and Christian "political correctness" so insistent that we follow
"modern interpretations". Do these people not know what is at
stake here? Here they are again:

◊ Creation – six literal days or otherwise?
◊ Israel – a prophetic or rejected entity?
◊ Salvation – Jesus, the only way to God?
◊ Hell – is it really as bleak as we are told?
◊ End Times – how are things going to be wrapped up?

These five battlegrounds have endured repeated conflict throughout
Christian history, fought by Greek and Hebrew antagonists. We
will now visit each in turn and watch the battles as they unfold
over history. By doing so we will get a handle on what Christians
have believed and, more importantly, why they have believed.

Two questions, though, should be scrawled on post-it notes in your mind's eye, to be constantly recalled:

1. What was Jesus' own understanding?
2. If Christians have deviated from this, what has influenced them to do so?

Do we accept that, while he was on Earth, Jesus had a perfect understanding of all areas we are considering? If we do so, then do we also accept that his understanding still holds? Do we hold Bible truths as timeless and as relevant now as they were 2000 years ago? Or do we consider that, for social, cultural, political or other reasons, the parameters have changed?

Let us allow the Bible to speak on this.

For the word of God is living and active. Sharper than any double-edged sword, it penetrates even to dividing soul and spirit, joints and marrow; it judges the thoughts and attitudes of the heart. (Hebrews 4:12)

Jesus Christ is the same yesterday and today and forever. (Hebrews 13:8)

For, "All men are like grass, and all their glory is like the flowers of the field; the grass withers and the flowers fall, but the word of the Lord stands forever." And this is the word that was preached to you. (1 Peter 1:24-25)
Heaven and earth will pass away, but my words will never pass away. (Matthew 24:35)
Your word, O LORD, is eternal; it stands firm in the heavens. (Psalm 119:89)

The Bible has spoken. It is now time for men to speak. Let the battles commence...

Has Darwin Made a Monkey Out of You?

For Christians it's the hottest chestnut of them all, so much so that most believers don't touch it for fear of getting their fingers burnt. To take one of the two traditional positions is to lay yourself open either to ridicule or righteous anger. Many take refuge in compromise, but is that just a cop-out? It's time we thought hard about this issue and did some research.

Abraham, Moses, Joshua and King Josiah all believed in a literal six day Creation. *Well of course they did, they had no evidence to believe anything else.* And there's the central issue: *evidence*. Evidence is defined as something that helps us to reach a conclusion. Let's take it a little further. Is the Bible a book to be open to new evidence? Was it God's plan to make the Bible pliable enough to allow for new interpretations as soon as mankind had new knowledge, or evidence, to re-evaluate things? Or is the Bible fixed in stone, plain in its interpretation and rigid and uncompromising in its message, regardless of the advances in human discoveries and thinking? We will return to those thoughts a little later on.

In those early "Days of Torah" at the time of Joshua, all believed that God created the World in six days. These stories would have been passed down from generation to generation. Dare we believe that they could even have been traced back to Adam regaling Seth and his other kids with stories of when he, himself, had spoken to God Himself, from the days when they walked together in the garden in the cool of the day?

Of course the Israelites were also exposed to other ideas. The Canaanites, like many ancient cultures, saw their gods and goddesses as forever fighting and procreating, primarily looking after their own interests and providing mankind with *incidental* benefits, such as the creation of the land, the sea and everything else. These crude imaginings just pale into total insignificance, when judged against the sheer majesty of Creation by the loving and all-powerful Father God of the Hebrews. It is very hard to believe the Children of Israel being seduced by these alternative scenarios, although undoubtedly some succumbed, seduced in a very real sense by the sexual aspects of the pagan worship to Baal and Astoreth.

By the time we arrive at the time of the Kings of Judah and Israel, the Hebrews would have been exposed to the Creation myths of all of the people who lived with them and alongside them. Some Babylonians believed in a fight between a young god, Marduk, and the ocean, which is defeated and split in two, providing the Earth and the sky. Man is subsequently created from the blood of one out of the defeated army. Sumerians put themselves at the centre of the Creation. One Egyptian myth has a god extruding bodily fluids, which became Earth and sky, born in a state of copulation! Another Egyptian myth involves an egg laid upon a mound of dirt by a heavenly bird.

But again, we must match these against the Biblical Creation story told at the start of Genesis. The Bible story alone is free of the human concerns of sex, war and national pride and just rings true, as a result. Without endowing the Creator with human characteristics or failings it provides the simple narrative of a holy, separate, benign and loving God speaking the Universe, the Earth, life and mankind into existence over a six day period.

We now progress to the days of the early Church. Jesus, as already mentioned, was a creationist by virtue of the fact that, as the Creator, he remembered the act of Creation.

He is the image of the invisible God, the firstborn over all creation. For by him all things were created: things in heaven and on earth, visible and invisible, whether thrones or powers or rulers or authorities; all things were created by him and for him. He is before all things, and in him all things hold together.
(Colossians 1:15-17)

There are other clues. First from the mouth of Jesus:

Therefore this generation will be held responsible for the blood of all the prophets that has been shed <u>since the beginning of the world</u>, from the blood of Abel to the blood of Zechariah, who was killed between the altar and the sanctuary. Yes, I tell you, this generation will be held responsible for it all.
(Luke 11:50-51)

Here Jesus places the affairs of man firmly *at the beginning of the World* i.e. quite soon after Creation. Then Paul seems to agree with this:

For <u>since the creation of the world</u> God's invisible qualities his eternal power and divine nature have been clearly seen, being understood from what has been made, so that men are without excuse.
(Romans 1:20)

It all seemed so straightforward in those very early days of the Church, the Jewish years, when Holy Scripture alone sufficed to provide one with a worldview. But then, along came the Greeks...

Returning to our view of Church history, you will remember Justin Martyr, one of the first Church Fathers. He was one of the first apologists, defenders of the faith, although his background, in common with the majority of these Fathers of the Church, was in Greek philosophy.

Justin queried the fact that Adam was told that the day he ate the forbidden fruit was the day he would die, yet he lived many hundreds of years. From this Justin made a logical jump and pulled out a Scripture (*But do not forget this one thing, dear friends: With the Lord a day is like a thousand years, and a thousand years are like a day.* 2 Peter 3:8) and proclaimed that perhaps days were not always 24 hour periods and hence the Days of Creation were not *literal* days.

So, already, doubt had set in. Let us move on to Clement of Alexandria, the first Christian philosopher to really push the ideas of Plato into the Church. What did he think of the Days of Creation? Well, unpack this... if you dare!

For the creations on the different days followed in a most important succession; so that all things brought into existence might have honour from priority, created together in thought, but not being of equal worth. Nor was the creation of each signified by the voice, inasmuch as the creative work is said to have made them at once. For something must needs have been named first. Wherefore those things were announced first, from which came those that were second, all things being originated together from one essence by one power. For the will of God was one, in one identity. And how could creation take place in time, seeing time was born along with things which exist.

(*The Stromata*, Book 6, Chapter 16).

Eh?! What Clement was saying was the idea, borrowed from Philo, an earlier Jewish philosopher and the first Biblical Platonist, that God did not actually create over a six day period, but created everything at the same time! The "days" were just put there to add an order of priority to things.

Then there was Origen, the father of *Christian allegory*, the Greek idea of assigning deeper meanings to literal texts. He writes:

What intelligent person can imagine that there was a first
"day," then a second and a third "day" [evening and
morning] without the sun, the moon, and the stars? And that
the first "day" [if it makes sense to call it such] existed even
without a sky? Who is foolish enough to believe that, like a
human gardener, God planted a garden in Eden in the East
and placed in it a tree of life, visible and physical, so that by
biting into its fruit one would obtain life? And that by eating
from another tree, one would come to know good and evil?
And when it is said that God walked in the garden in the
evening and that Adam hid himself behind a tree, I cannot
imagine that anyone will doubt that these details point
symbolically to spiritual meanings, by using an historical
narrative which did not literally happen.

(Origen's *"De Principiis"* 4.1.6)

Well, he couldn't have explained himself clearer in his utter rejection of any literal understanding of not just the Days of Creation, but the Adam and Eve story too. For him, the whole story should be read solely for their deeper meanings and symbolism.

What about the man mostly acknowledged as the Father of Western Christianity? What did Augustine have to say? Actually this issue concerned him quite a lot and wrote much on the subject, including in his *Confessions, The City of God* and *the Literal Meaning of Genesis.*

The gist of his thinking is that, just as with Clement, he believed that God brought everything into existence instantaneously and that the Days of Creation are just a commentary on this, to be examined allegorically. He also believed in a concept of evolution, with God allowing part of His creation to develop and evolve independently but always under His control.

Interestingly these Church Fathers had no problem with the capacity of God to create the World, the Universe and everything in such a short time. Their argument was that six days was too long a time and surely God would have done His work instantaneously.

The reason why they said this was fundamentally the same reason that many modern Christians have trouble with a literal Six Days and that is *physical evidence*. Nowadays it's the Theory of Evolution that provides the stumbling block, but in their day it was human logic and understanding. As Origen said,

> *What intelligent person can imagine that there was a first "day," then a second and a third "day"—evening and morning—without the sun, the moon, and the stars? And that the first "day"—if it makes sense to call it such—existed even without a sky?*

So, let's analyse. Origen is appealing here to *human intelligence*. But since when has human intelligence brought us understanding of divine motivations? Yes, that did sound a bit clunky and self-defeating, but what I mean to say is that, to human intelligence, many fundamental events in the Bible are impossible. The sun standing still for Joshua and the Red Sea parting for Moses, for instance. How logical are these? When the impossible happens, we move out of the realm of *human intelligence*, into God's realm of the supernatural. So if God can speak of a "day" before He's even created the sun, moon and stars, then He must have a rather good reason.

It's useful at this point to ask the question that Origen and Augustine should have been asking, *why did God choose to take so long to create everything?* It's a good question, because God certainly could have created everything in a single moment, but He chose not to. Why?

God speaks to us through His actions. Everything He does has a reason and it is our task to discover that reason. It's not an easy task for us Westernised Christians brought up with a Greek mind-set, a way of thinking totally divorced from the Hebrew mind-set of those who lived in Bible times.

I will speak of one reason. God wanted to set us a pattern, a model for the working week, six days of work followed by a day of rest.

*For in six days the LORD made the heavens and the earth, the
sea, and all that is in them, but he rested on the seventh day.
Therefore the LORD blessed the Sabbath day and made it holy.*
(Exodus 20:11)

He set the pattern by example and, if we know what is good for us,
we follow Him.

Now these Christian philosophers, from Justin to Augustine, had
no real evidence with which to re-interpret the first two chapters of
Genesis. They had no Charles Darwin rattling his bones at them. Why
did most of them think that God couldn't have spoken everything
into existence over six days? Were they already analyzing Him,
judging Him by the same criteria that they applied to the exploits
of man? Did the works of God just seem inconceivable to the mind
of man? If so, then the Grand Folly had begun... the squeezing of
God into a man-sized box.

How did this pan out as we move into the Medieval Church?
In our historical overview, the next key Christian thinker on our
journey was Thomas Aquinas, the most important and influential
Christian philosopher of the Middle Ages. What did the "dumb ox"
think about the Six Days of Creation?

Now Thomas was very much a Christian *philosopher*, with
a great inclination towards the thinking of Aristotle. So the idea
of a literal Six Day Creation was not going to go by unnoticed,
particularly for someone very interested in the interface between
reason and faith. His take is to offer the suggestion that, in a sense,
all things were created at the same time, in a *potential* sense. He
said, in Summa Theologica:

*On the day on which God created the heaven and the earth,
He created also every plant of the field, not, indeed, actually,
but "before it sprung up in the earth," that is, potentially.*

He adds to this by suggesting that God created the *substance* of
everything at the moment of Creation, even if they didn't actually
appear at the same time. This is all pure Aristotle and is a good

example of how theologians of every age have dipped their toes, if not their whole foot, into the murky waters of Greek philosophy. In fact, by dressing up his thoughts with such vague flowery language Thomas made it very unclear if he did actually believe in a literal Six Days of Creation.

Following Aquinas, the general position of the medieval Church on this issue was the position held by Augustine and the other Platonists, with an instantaneous Creation and the Six Days being allegorised, viewed more as poetic literature than literal commentary. Then came the *Reformation* and everything changed.

For a start their rallying cry was *Sola Scriptura*, scripture alone! Martin Luther, the prime mover, had this to say about the allegorical methods of Augustine:

"Augustine trifles with the six days in a strange way, making them days of hidden meaning, according to the knowledge of angels, and does not let them be six natural days."

(Commentary on Genesis, 2 vols., 4.)

The Reformers had wrenched the Bible from its self-appointed guardians, brushed off the dust from its cover and encouraged the ordinary Christian to read it. Bearing in mind that the ordinary Christian had no idea how to read Holy Scripture, being so culturally and historically divorced from the Hebrew authors of the book, Luther and his chums provided tools that would extract spiritual truths from the book. These were the *Grammatical Historic method* mentioned in the previous chapter, the idea of putting oneself in the role of someone who would have heard the words in the original setting and how they would have understood the words in context. They insisted that, in the first instance, one should look at the plain meaning sense of the Bible text, a very *Hebraic* idea.

So whereas the Catholics of their day had provided fanciful explanations for the meaning of the Six Days of Creation, the Reformers took God's word for it. If He said that He created everything in six actual days, then that would be good enough for them. In modern-day jargon, they were *Six Day Young Earth*

Creationists. *"We assert that Moses spoke in the literal sense, not allegorically or figuratively, i.e., that the world, with all its creatures, was created within six days, as the words read"*, said Luther (Lectures in Genesis: chapters 1-5).

Then came the *Enlightenment* and it all changed, again. Human reason held sway and advances in science made great inroads into how Christians began to see God and His Creation. Many Christians were torn, pulled apart by conflicting voices. On the one hand there was Archbishop Usher declaring that, as a result of his Biblical research, the Earth was created on October 26th, 4004 BC at 9am. On the other hand the *uniformitarians* had arrived. These were not Nazis that liked to dress up (bad joke) but rather a scientific concept that assumed that the universe's natural laws had never changed and that "the present is the key to the past". It all sounds quite innocuous until you realise that any literal Six Days of Creation wouldn't fit in as this would have been a one-off event, confounding the "natural laws of the universe" and in no way corresponds with the way the World works today.

So those Christians who were beginning to fall away from the faith through the pressures from both inside and outside the Church, at last had fuel to fan the flames of their doubt. These folk were now free to re-look at Genesis chapters one and two and felt they had proof, from the world of science, particularly Geology, to interpret the Days of Creation as longer periods of time. Now, it wasn't the Platonic allegory of Augustine that did the damage, but rather the scientific rationalism of Aristotle. So the Days of Creation were not viewed so much as poetry or symbolism but rather as just longer periods of time. These people were still, by and large, Creationists, but *Old Earth* Creationists, looking at millions of years, rather than Young Earth Creationists, looking at thousands of years since Creation.

Many Christians were beginning to falter in their faith. They still believed in the Resurrection, the minimum requirement for Christian belief, but now human reason had taken over from divine revelation as the dominant force in society. Human reason, rationalism, was the response to the dogmas of the Church and the pointless religious wars of recent years and science took a firm foothold on the minds of the great thinkers of the day. God was relegated from an active role in the affairs of man, to the One who kick-started the Universe then left it alone. Nothing was considered exempt from this process and the Bible found itself re-examined, God's written revelation was subjected to analysis by the human mind. It was called *Higher Criticism*. In the first edition (1771) of Encyclopedia Britannica, the entry for Noah's Ark included much musing over the finer details of the Biblical account of the Flood. In the ninth edition (1875) these had disappeared, no longer considered worthy of inclusion, the account having moved from Biblical account to mythology. That was the fruit of *Higher Criticism*.

It was within these changing times that a man appeared on a white charger as an embodiment of this new thinking. Charles Darwin was that man and his book, *"On the Origin of Species by Means of Natural Selection, or the Preservation of Favoured Races in the Struggle for Life"* proved a rallying point for rationalists, intellectuals and even many Christians to declare the victory of the mind over the spirit, of naturalism over supernaturalism. What did Darwin do? He must have been significant because even now, 150 years later in 2009, we celebrated "Darwin Day", our Natural History Museum is a shrine to the man, and the BBC is churning out hours of radio and TV dedicated to his ideas.

What Darwin did was to provide a scientific methodology to disengage mankind from the influence of the Bible. What had been considered as certainties could now be dismissed as myths, legends or poetry as discoveries and theories, interpreted by the rational mind of the scientist, began to take centre stage. The clincher came a few decades later at the infamous Scopes "monkey" trial, when a clever prosecutor managed to ridicule the ill-prepared Baptist minister and the theory of evolution firmly cemented itself in the Christian psyche as the most *reasonable* explanation for life on Earth. For Creationism, the prevalent view before Darwin, it was a long slippery path, certainly in the UK, into ridicule, denigration and bitterness. Creationists are now portrayed as simple-minded innocents at best or religious lunatics at worst. How could it have come to this? How can Christians fall out so spectacularly?

If you took a straw poll of any group of British Christians and asked them their views on this issue, the vast majority would say something like this: *I believe in the Bible and that God created life on Earth, but we surely need to marry this up with the overwhelming scientific evidence of the evolutionary process.* This is a reasonable view, after all. But then we must ask ourselves whether, as Christians, we are governed primarily by "reasonable" views... or Biblical revelation. In our scientific age, with our secular education and fed by our humanistic media, it is safest to take refuge in a majority view, held by those we have grown to respect, from David Attenborough to the BBC. Clever people have assured us that evolution is a done deal, the answer to everything. That is why there was a Darwin Day in 2009. Inasmuch as the human heart requires explanations of the World in which we live, the theory of evolution is the closest we have come to a secular religion. Darwin is the secular messiah and Dawkins and his ilk are his prophets. This is what many have bought into.

The trouble is that evolution as an explanation of the origin of life on Earth seems to be inconsistent with a Biblical worldview and a Christian view of the attributes of God and any attempt to shoe-horn it into Holy Scripture can be seen as a fudge and a compromise. To illustrate this, I ask just one question. Did Adam and Eve actually exist? The apostle Paul certainly thought so.

So it is written: "The first man Adam became a living being"; the last Adam, a life-giving spirit.
(1 Corinthians 15:45)

And so did Jesus.

But at the beginning of creation God 'made them male and female.'
(Mark 10:6)

But what about you, what do you think? Can the Bible be trusted in every way, or do we just pick and choose what to believe in, swayed by the prejudices and cleverness of others. The Bible genealogies suggest that Adam's grandson was a contemporary of Noah. So if Adam was not flesh and blood, then what about Noah, was he a legendary figure and the Flood just a myth or an allegory? Noah's own son, Shem, lived at the time of Abraham, the father of our faith, so could they have actually met? Or is Abraham just another legend, in which case who exactly decides when fables give way to actual history? Or, putting it another way, when does that great gallery of faithful ones in Hebrews 11 switch from fiction to fact? And if Abraham's existence is questionable, then that takes us into very dangerous waters indeed. If the foundations of your faith are shaky then on what basis are you secure in your salvation?

I contend that our Christian faith depends on the fact that Adam was flesh and blood. A real man had to eat from the tree of knowledge of good and evil and bring about that curse on mankind known as the Fall, the falling away from God and the need for redemption, bought for us by the death and resurrection of another real man (of divine origin), whose existence we don't doubt, Jesus Christ. Adam sinned and, as the Bible tells us, death came into the World.

Therefore, just as sin entered the world through one man, and death through sin, and in this way death came to all men, because all sinned.
(Romans 5:12)

If death came into the World through Adam and Eve, then what about the dinosaurs, crocodiles and mammoths that supposedly pre-dated them in the billions of years since the first cell was created by some chemical accident? How do you explain their deaths if death hadn't yet entered the World? How do you explain the cancers and other diseases that these animals suffered, if the Fall hadn't yet occurred? There are a lot of questions that need to be answered. Scenarios have been put forward by Christians attempting to marry evolutionary theory with Scripture. Some put the millions of years required by the theory of evolution in between the first two days of Creation, others put them later in Creation week. They say they are being consistent with Scripture, but they still fail to explain how death had crept in before the Fall. Still others accept the full secular deal and concede a full animal ancestry! To these people we need to ask, *what is your starting point, the Bible or science?*

If science is our starting point we are saying that our frame of reference is the constantly developing world of the scientist, the world of reason. If the Bible is our starting point, then it is the *unchanging* Word of God, the source of revelation. When these two worlds seem to clash, as Christians we either stand or fall by the Word of God, without compromise, even if we are vilified by others, even brothers and sisters in Christ!

Six days, six days, I ask you! From billions of years to six days! You're asking too much of me! Yes, it seems unreasonable, of course it does. Yet many scientists, proper scientists with doctorates and academic success, are Creationists and have answered all the objections that evolutionists have put in their way and provided reasonable alternatives for their beliefs that don't compromise the Word of God. Despite what others may say, a belief in Creationism is not unreasonable, irrational or ignorant.

But the virgin birth and the resurrection are unreasonable, yet we accept them as truth. How big is your God? Do you struggle to fit Him into the box marked "miracles of Jesus"? If you can live with this then just consider Jesus' *other* miracles. The reason why Jesus himself believed in a six day creation was because he was the one who did the creating! He was around at that time. Were Dawkins or Darwin around too? So who better to believe, an active eyewitness or an atheist postulator of theories?

> *"In the beginning was the Word, and the Word was with God, and the Word was God. He was with God in the beginning. Through him all things were made; without him nothing was made that has been made."* (John 1:1-3)

Make no mistake, evolution is the religion of our age and it serves a jealous "god" that is most definitely not the God of Abraham, Isaac and Jacob. It not only tells us that life came about through blind chance and that we are descended from apes, but it has insinuated itself into our consciousness, through our educational, legal, communication and – sad to say – ecclesiastical systems. It tells us that as life itself was a random chance, then our lives are random too. It has no room for absolutes, governed only by its rule of survival of the fittest. It makes abortion and euthanasia acceptable and finds its perfect expression in totalitarian regimes, like Nazi Germany or Soviet Russia, where individual freedoms are sacrificed for the good of the majority, because individual lives are considered worthless.

Charles Darwin was groomed by his father to be a clergyman and, in his own words, "*did not then in the least doubt the strict and literal truth of every word in the Bible.*" His life, of course, followed a very different path, one that destroyed that faith, to the extent that, in a letter to a correspondent shortly before his death, wrote "*I am sorry to have to inform you that I do not believe in the Bible as a divine revelation, and therefore not in Jesus Christ as the Son of God.*" So Darwin's life work on formulating the theory of evolution was to lose him his faith in Father God.

It's all really down to a concept that I sketched out in my previous book, that of roots and agendas. Basically, all Christians have a shared agenda. We all believe in what Jesus has done for us and the teachings that we must follow as a consequence. Now every agenda has an underlying cause, a *root*. In this example the root is the work of the Holy Spirit in our lives.

But there can be other agendas in the Body of Christ, let's call them *secondary* agendas. The path dictated by my Jewish background became my agenda. Others follow different paths and agendas because we all have different roots. Your family could be lifelong Methodists, Anglicans, Baptists or Catholics (or any one of hundreds of others) and, through your formative years, you would have taken on board many of their teachings and customs.

You could have a Muslim, Jewish or Hindu background, then there is the matter of your lifestyle or personal philosophy before your conversion. You could have lived a hedonistic lifestyle of debauchery and self-fulfilment. You could have been a communist, a conservative, a green activist, a vegetarian, an animal liberationist, a feminist, a homosexual, even an atheist. You may have been a naturally spiritual person, or a rationalist, even a hardened sceptic. These are our roots. Even before God comes into our lives, we all still have a set of beliefs, even if it is just a self-belief.

Then God hits us with the gospel, opens up our minds and hearts and leads us into an incredible adventure as a New Creation. His intention, I believe, is to take the raw material and mould us into something new and wonderful. In some cases, the master potter uses some old clay, parts of our "old creation", as He re-constructs us from inside out. But we are not inanimate objects, lifeless jars of clay, but are allowed to retain that most precious of gifts, our free will. By ensuring that we continue to act as individuals within the great worldwide network of the Body of Christ, it also opens us up to a danger. It is the temptation of individualism, perhaps allowing too much of our past lives to season our present and future lives. In these cases the root could act as a catalyst for disruption. It's a possibility and sometimes we need others to tell us if this is so.

So, we need to honestly examine our root and the agenda that flows from it. The issue of Creation is a battleground because, perhaps more than any other current issue, it divides Christians.

Those who cling on to the ancient belief in a literal Six Day Creation are considered by the others as eccentric, ignorant, primitive, even an embarrassment. I witnessed a TV debate recently when a former Archbishop of Canterbury turned on a Creationist, a fellow Christian brother and stated that he felt he had more in common with the atheist scientist sitting opposite him in the studio. Some have even declared Creationists as a hindrance to the gospel. My answer to that is to ask, *what gospel are they referring to? Is it the gospel of Jesus Christ or a variation of the same, but acceptable to thinking rational people?!*

Frankly it is very difficult to be a Creationist in today's climate. To the secularists it is a joke and flies in the face of acceptable wisdom and the bedrock philosophy of our society. It is an affront to the theory of evolution, that holds together our educational, scientific and communication systems with the same certainty and influence as Catholicism held together medieval society. To other Christians, even those who have succumbed to a compromised version of Creationism, it is *spiritual incorrectness*, to be avoided wherever possible.

Now let's consider agendas. If we are Six Day Creationists then we are following the agenda of the first Church, of the Reformers, as well as Charles Spurgeon, John Wesley, Martyn Lloyd-Jones and many others. But more than all this, we are following the agenda of the One who was there at Creation, Jesus Christ.

If we trust Jesus on so many issues and rely on him unswervingly for our very salvation, why can't we trust him on this issue? Jesus is the same yesterday, today and forever. The same cannot be said for the world of science, which is *never the same* yesterday, today and forever, because scientists are forever changing their explanations of the World around them!

Unlike our Saviour, scientists were not present at Creation, they can only make assumptions. No theory is provable without observable evidence and so everything is guesswork. Science, as I said, is never the same, it is always moving, changing, re-evaluating... evolving! Here's a quote from a famous scientist and philosopher, Karl Popper.

If we are uncritical we shall always find what we want:
we shall look for and find confirmations and we shall look
away from and not see whatever might be dangerous to our
pet theories.

Do we trust our Christian worldview in the hands of these people? Is that what defines your agenda? Is your agenda primarily driven by your *rationalism*, inherited from the days of the Enlightenment, using the analytical methods devised by such as Aristotle? Are we

Christians who are forever balancing the unchanging truths of the Bible against the evidence fed to us by science? If so, how do we make the call, where do we draw the line between revealed truth and contrary evidence? Science tells us that the sun cannot be stopped in its path, that virgins don't give birth, that men can't walk on water, that seas don't part, that water can't turn to wine, that lepers can't be healed, that men cannot rise from the dead, that God can't create the World, the Universe and everything in six days. Have you lined up your dominoes yet?

These are heavy statements, but the only way to really understand them is to take things back a stage. We must look at the root that is driving our agenda. If you are a Six Day Creationist, believing in the literal Creation of everything in six days according to the Book of Genesis, then that is your agenda and the root of your agenda is *your faith in God's Word alone*. It's not an easy position, it is the vulnerable under-belly, open to attack from the scientific rationalism that defines our age, which is why it is a minority position in today's Church.

Most Christians have to accept ridicule from their non-believing friends in their stance over Jesus rising from the dead after three days and then appearing and disappearing over a six week period before being whisked to Heaven in a cloud. For any born-again Christian this is non-negotiable, it's the bedrock of our faith, the absolute minimum requirement. We are declaring a belief in supernatural events, events beyond nature, inexplicable by science. We hold to these truths as Christians, through *our faith in God's Word*, yet our rational mind screams at us the impossibility of what we believe in. That's what faith is all about, *being certain of what we do not see* (Hebrews 11).

Yet most of these same Christians turn to their Creationist friends and say to them, *you can't be serious believing in all that nonsense!* And when challenged, their only defence is what science has told them, indirectly through the media and the education system. There is no ready defence of their position within the pages of the Bible.

Is this your agenda? If so, then we must examine the root of your agenda. Could this be *doubt*, pure and simple? No, you haven't condemned yourself, you haven't stopped being a Christian, Jesus still loves you. But something may have crept in, something from *outside* of revealed truth. Something enticing, authoritative and convincing but, nevertheless, *still* from outside of revealed truth.

If any of you lacks wisdom, he should ask God, who gives generously to all without finding fault, and it will be given to him. But when he asks, he must believe and not doubt, because he who doubts is like a wave of the sea, blown and tossed by the wind.
(James 1:5-6)

This has to be the key passage on this issue. Meditate on this, then ask God to reveal to you if you do *lack wisdom*. If you believe He is speaking to you, then ask for this wisdom in complete faith, even allowing for the possibility that you could have been wrong and have been deflected from the truth. Don't take my word for it, as I am just a mortal man with his own ideas. You must always leave the last word to the Lord Himself.

Choices, Choices!

Surely it's reasonable to think that, having given His first people chance after chance after chance and watching them fail, then fail again, then fail even more, that God would draw a line and say *enough is enough, it's time to move on.* After all, didn't they shed the blood of God's prophets, from Abel to Zechariah? Didn't they bow to the Baals, worship at the Asherah poles, sacrifice their children to Moloch? Didn't they turn the back on His laws and statutes, even God Himself, despite all He did for them throughout their early history? And, worst of all, didn't they kill God's own son?

Surely justice demands action. God had every right not just to move His affections to His *new* covenant people, but to demand that His new partners, the Church, should commence a 2000 year campaign of persecution, to ensure that the Jews would be thoroughly punished for their behaviour and be in no doubt of their status as an utterly rejected people.

This may seem an unfair observation and a distortion of God's character, but the outworking of the Church's attitude to the Jews is true history. The treatment of the Jewish people by the established Church from the 2nd Century onwards has arguably been the grossest distortion of God's aspirations ever conceived by the mind of man.

We now travel back in time but, before we do so, it is worth considering the following questions:

Do you believe the Jewish nation is eternally cursed as a result of their rejection of Jesus? Do you believe they have forfeited their right to be the "chosen people"? Do you believe that Christians have supplanted the Jewish people as the only "people of God"?

We will consider these questions again later.

A good place to start would be to ask what Jesus had to say about his people, with regard to their future and their standing before God, his Father. But we will not be doing that here. Instead we will allow the historical Church to demonstrate its views, by its actions, and then we will consider whether we believe Jesus would have sanctioned these views.

We begin shortly after the death of the last Jewish apostle, John the Evangelist. Remembering the Church Fathers we met in chapter four, we begin with Ignatius of Antioch, probably one of John's disciples. He wrote a letter to the church in Magnesia, which included some comments about the Jews.

Never allow yourselves to be led astray by false teachings and antiquated and useless fables. Nothing of any use can be got from them. If we are still living in the practice of Judaism, it is an admission that we have failed to receive the gift of grace... To profess Jesus Christ while continuing to follow Jewish customs is an absurdity. The Christian faith does not look to Judaism, but Judaism looks to Christianity...

Now before we scream "anti-Semitism", we need to know the context of the letter. Ignatius was concerned with the Jewish people in Magnesia who had become believers in Jesus, but were still clinging a little too much to the "old ways". Now this can be looked at in two ways. Either these Jews were adhering so much to the rules and regulations imposed by the Rabbis that they failed to make Jesus the centre of their worship, or they were simply living out their new faith in the best way they could, but in a Jewish context. Either way, it was clear that they were beginning to upset their Gentile Christian neighbours, so much so that they demanded instruction from one of the foremost Christian leaders of the day. Warning signs indeed of worse to come.

Justin Martyr, living early in the 2nd Century AD, was the first to provide the fuel for the unhappy days to follow. He wrote *Dialogue with Trypho*, a theological boxing match with a Jew, where the victor gets to write the book! It is a dangerous book, filled with naked attacks on both the Jews and their beliefs. He blames the Jews for the crucifixion and gloats at what he saw as their just punishment.

> *All this has happened to you rightly and well, For ye slew*
> *the Just One and His prophets before Him, and now ye*
> *reject, and... dishonor those who set their hopes on Him, and*
> *God Almighty and Maker of the universe who sent Him...*

So what do we make of this? Remember, the last of Jesus' Jewish apostles had died not too long earlier and the Jewish Christian community had dwindled by this time to a negligible number. Justin had felt sufficiently confident in his reading of both the "Signs of the Times" and Holy Scripture to orchestrate such an attack on the Jews.

Yet what were his justifications? Blaming the Jews for the death of Christ shows an appalling lack of understanding of Biblical truths and. Here are six reasons why:

1. It was the Romans who actually killed Jesus. Crucifixion was a Roman instrument of death.

2. It was the Jewish leadership who bore the responsibility for the rejection of Jesus, not the Jews as a whole (Matthew 27:20).

3. Jesus had to die for Christianity to exist. There could be no resurrection without a crucifixion. Is it fair to eternally condemn whoever is responsible for this part in God's plan for mankind?

4. On the cross Jesus himself forgave the people responsible for his death (Luke 23:34). He also laid down his life willingly.

5. Jesus knew in advance of his death; he spoke of it earlier to his disciples. It was no surprise to him. (John 10:17-18)

6. It was all God's idea in the first place! (Acts 2:23)

Even if God was so filled with holy wrath that He would want to wipe out the Jews for their failure and faithlessness, *who* set the Church up as judge, jury and executioner!? As Jesus said:

"Do not judge, and you will not be judged. Do not condemn, and you will not be condemned. Forgive, and you will be forgiven."
(Luke 6:37)

According to Justin and those who followed, the Jews had now blown it; they had lost their *chosenness,* and this honour now belonged to the Church, the new "spiritual Israel". This is known as *Replacement Theology* or *Supercessionism.* Justin says as much in his *Dialogue with Trypho*:

We have been led to God through this crucified Christ,
and we are the true spiritual Israel, and the descendants
of Judah, Jacob, Isaac, and Abraham, who, though
uncircumcised, was approved and blessed by God because of
his faith and was called the father of many nations. All this
will be proved as we proceed with our discussion.

Spiritual Israel? Where does that come from? Is this in the Bible? It isn't, unless you want it to be there. It suited the orderly Greek minds of the time to make assumptions and logical leaps, interpreting Holy Scripture in the light of their own ideas and expectations. It also smacked of Plato's dualism, which cast the Jews as the inferior and rejected "physical" people of the Old Covenant and Christians as the superior and blessed "spiritual" people of the New Covenant. Yet the Bible speaks otherwise:

I do not want you to be ignorant of this mystery, brothers, so that
you may not be conceited: Israel has experienced a hardening in

part until the full number of the Gentiles has come in. And so all
Israel will be saved…
(Romans 11:25-26)

Of course the Church Father, Origen, with his allegorical way of
interpreting Holy Scripture, would feel that he had every right to
believe the Church was the Spiritual Israel. After all, Plato would
have been in full agreement with this idea. To Origen (and to Plato
if he had still been alive), the Jews were *earthly* people, crude,
hard-hearted, materialistic murderers. He would have agreed with
what Justin Martyr had said:

> *But you were never shown to be possessed of friendship or*
> *love either towards God, or towards the prophets, or towards*
> *yourselves, but, as is evident, you are ever found to be*
> *idolaters and murderers of righteous men, so that you laid*
> *hands even on Christ Himself; and to this very day you abide*
> *in your wickedness, execrating those who prove that this man*
> *who was crucified by you is the Christ.*
>
> (Dialogue with Trypho, 93)

In Origen's mind, the physical, materialistic, law-strangled Jews
were to be contrasted with the spiritually-minded grace-abounding
Christians. This dualism split the Bible in two and relegated the
Jews to a role as the rejected people of the past.

Replacement Theology is a perfect expression of the ideas of
Plato; its followers should be proud of themselves for integrating
pagan Greek philosophy into their Christian beliefs!

Origen digs the knife in even further.

> *On account of their unbelief and other insults which they*
> *heaped upon Jesus, the Jews will not only suffer more than*
> *others in the judgment which is believed to impend over the*
> *world, but have even already endured such sufferings. For*
> *what nation is in exile from their own metropolis, and from*
> *the place sacred to the worship of their fathers, save the*

Jews alone? And the calamities they have suffered because
they were a most wicked nation, which although guilty of
many other sins, yet has been punished so severely for none
as for those that were committed against our Jesus.

(Against Celsus)

But the worst was to come. It came from the greatest preacher of
his day, a man so respected for his flowing inspirational oratory that
he was called the Golden-mouthed. This was John Chrysostom,
the 4th Century Archbishop of Constantinople. Earlier in his career,
in a series of eight sermons, the *Adversus Judaeos*, he produced a
vitriolic attack against the Jews that would have done Hitler proud.

But the synagogue is not only a brothel and a theater; it also
is a den of robbers and a lodging for wild beasts... when
God forsakes a people, what hope of salvation is left? When
God forsakes a place, that place becomes the dwelling of
demons.

(I III 1).

They live for their bellies, they gape for the things of this
world, their condition is not better than that of pigs or goats
because of their wanton ways and excessive gluttony. They
know but one thing: to fill their bellies and be drunk, to get
all cut and bruised, to be hurt and wounded while fighting
for their favorite charioteers.

(I IV 1).

Yet this was no demonic dictator, this was *John the Golden-mouthed.*
His words were considered, planned and intentional. The effects of
his words, though, for the Jews, were significant, disastrous and
fatal. He was a highly respected leader of the Christian Church, *he*
had to be right, didn't he?

Ironically, it seems that one reason for this attack was that the
Jews were becoming too successful in swaying Christians away
from Church practices. In short, the Christianity of the State Church

was so unattractive that the customs and beliefs of Judaism were becoming quite alluring. Some were taking part in Jewish festivals, keeping Sabbath, even being circumcised. John even claimed that some women were visiting synagogues during the festivals, because of their love for the solemnity of the liturgy. Of course this practise was eventually kicked into touch through proclamations of various Church Councils, prohibiting Christians in the most severe manner from continuing in these activities.

Whatever motives John may have had, the end result was that he normalised *Christian anti-Semitism* for centuries to come. Augustine, the Father of Western Christianity, as the inheritor of Greek thought from Origen, was also convinced that the Church had replaced the Jews in God's plans. But he had a different slant on what to do about it. After hearing about the pogrom in Alexandria, when "Christians", fired up by the theological rabble-rousing by their Church leaders, slaughtered many Jews, Augustine said *no, don't kill the Jews!*

What's this? Had Christendom thrown up a true friend and protector of the Jews? Sadly, not; Augustine had a plan. He figured out that their punishment for their rejection of Jesus would be more effective if they were kept alive but never allowed to thrive. So perhaps the bittersweet survival of the Jews through the turbulent times of Christendom has been mainly down to Augustine!

By contrast, Thomas Aquinas seemed to have had little effect on the treatment of Jews, which by then had reached alarming levels. There were the pogroms throughout Europe and the Middle East as a result of the Crusades, the violence that resulted from superstitious lies concerning Jews, the blood libels and host desecrations, the seizing of Jewish properties and the expulsions that saw Jews ping-ponging to and fro between one hostile European "Christian" state and another.

The fierce and unforgiving attitude towards the Jews from their "Christian" neighbours was a direct result of the theological conclusions of their teachers and preachers, from Justin Martyr, Origen and John Chrysostom, through to Augustine and Aquinas.

Justin set the ball rolling by providing justification of their rejection as "Christ-killers", then Origen "proved" their replacement by the Church theologically, followed by John Chrysostom's call to action against this *rejected* people. Augustine ensured their survival, albeit as a people living on the margins of society and Thomas Aquinas did nothing to change the status-quo in his work on creating a theological structure for the Christian faith. Perhaps, with the Reformers, things would change?

Luther makes a bold proclamation. *"Let's start reading our Bibles"*, he says. He reads his Bible and discovers that Jesus was Jewish. He writes a pamphlet, *That Jesus Christ was born a Jew* (1523), which affirms the Jewish descent of Jesus. He denounces the wickedness of popes and priests in their attitude to Jews. He advocates a loving attitude to them, to win them to Christianity. But…

Twenty years later. He was near the end of his life. He'd achieved much, founded a Church, helped found a major religious movement.

But very few Jews had converted to Christianity!

Martin Luther's love turned to hate. He changed his attitude towards Jews. He became hostile to them and issued a new set of pamphlets, one of them titled *On the Jews and their Lies* (1543). Within these writings we can read words he used to describe these people he once wrote so favourably about: *"venomous… thieves… disgusting vermin… a pestilence and misfortune for our country… children of the devil ."*

He proposed the following remedies:

1. Set fire to their synagogues.

2. Homes should be broken down and destroyed.

3. Deprive them of their sacred books.

4. Rabbis should be forbidden to teach.

5. Passport and travelling privileges withdrawn.

6. Stop them from moneylending (although it was the only 'acceptable' trade for them).

7. Give them hard physical labour.

His conclusion was this: *"To sum up, dear princes and nobles who have Jews in your domains, if this advice of mine does not suit you, then find a better one so that you may all be free of this insufferable devilish burden – The Jews."*

"Find a better one?"

These were prophetic words indeed, particularly when we consider the legacy of this German preacher; in *"Mein Kampf"*, a book that needs no introduction, we read that Luther was one of Hitler's heroes.

But was Martin Luther typical of the Reformers? Actually, no. He seemed to have had unique problems with Jews. John Calvin, the other great Founding Father of the Reformers, said:

> *I extend the word Israel to all the people of God, according to this meaning, When the Gentiles shall come in, the Jews also shall return from their defection to the obedience of faith; and thus shall be completed the salvation of the whole Israel of God, which must be gathered from both; and yet in such a way that the Jews shall obtain the first place, being as it were the first born in God's family.*

(Commentaries Vol. 19)

Although the renewed importance of the Bible brought dividends in the form of a proper understanding of the relationship between God and the Jewish people, anti-Semitism still pervaded the Church, both Catholic and Protestant.

Apparently sliding off on a tangent I would like to draw your attention to the following list of first names; William, John, Thomas,

Richard, David, Daniel, Abraham, Jonas, Nathaniel and Samuel. These were the most popular boy's names in the Jamestown, Virginia colony which was established in 1607 in the land that was eventually to become the USA. What is remarkable about this list is that the last six names are Jewish names straight out of the Old Testament. So were 60% of the settlers Jewish? No, they were those Reformers within the Reformers. They were *Puritans*. Here were a people utterly devoted to the Word of God and aimed to follow it in the creation of the perfect society. As a template for this they took the model of ancient Israel, Old Testament Israel.

So what was going on here? Were the Puritans, so influential in bringing Jews back to England after a four century exile, at the forefront of a new Christian movement that was to be a blessing to the Jews? Yes and no.

Was it that, through their exhaustive reading of the Bible, they empathised with the Jews? They certainly did nothing to add to the "Christian" bile and phlegm of anti-Jewish hatred, but they added a new slant that is still with us in modern times. They so identified with Old Testament culture that they took on a lot of its trappings, from a love of Hebrew to the use of Jewish names. One reason for this was the need to see the Jews saved (and returning to their ancestral land), because only then, they thought, would Jesus Christ return. How better to do so than make Christianity more attractive for them, by showing a positive attitude to Jewish culture and religious practices. So it wasn't exactly motivated by love; there was a selfish element, albeit with a positive by-product of saved Jewish souls.

And thus has been the Jewish lot in their relationship with the Church. Although there have been times where genuine love for the Jews has been expressed by individual Christians, especially over the last couple of centuries, in general the pendulum has swung between self-righteous hatred and selfish theological ambition.

Returning to our historical survey we ask ourselves whether Catholic (and Protestant) anti-Semitism lessened as the official Church began to lose its iron grip on individual Christians. As we enter the Age of "Enlightenment" certainly the movement of individuals, from both within and without the Church, in favour of the Jews returning to their land, started to gain ground. The literal promises of God to Abraham and his descendants were beginning to touch hearts.

> *On that day the LORD made a covenant with Abram and said, "To your descendants I give this land, from the river of Egypt to the great river, the Euphrates -- the land of the Kenites, Kenizzites, Kadmonites, Hittites, Perizzites, Rephaites, Amorites, Canaanites, Girgashites and Jebusites."*
> (Genesis 15:18-20)

The list of individuals was an impressive one, including John Milton, John Locke, Isaac Newton, Joseph Priestly, Lord Shaftesbury, William Wilberforce, Charles Spurgeon, John Calvin, Jonathan Edwards, George Eliot and Lord Balfour, to name just a few. The movement was called Christian Zionism and it is still with us today.

But old hatreds still remained. Pogroms and massacres continued. Periodic persecutions of Jews continued until the late 18th Century and anti-Semitism still continued, but in a different form. As *reason* took over from faith, Jews were not only accused of being "Christ-killers", but for "inventing" Christianity itself and, ironically, causing the injustices and cruelty committed by followers of "religion". Some of the most prominent, such as Voltaire, ridiculed the Jews as a group alienated from society who practiced a primitive and superstitious religion.

With the emergence of nationalism as the defining factor in European society in the 19th Century, anti-Semitism acquired a *racial* rather than a religious character and Jews, with their differences, were regarded as aliens in society. Dodgy scientific theories asserting that the Jews were inferior to the so-called Aryan "races" gave anti-Semitism new respectability and popular support, especially in countries where Jews could be made scapegoats for existing social or political grievances. In this new climate, anti-Semitism became a powerful political tool, as politicians were quick to discover. In both Germany and Austria in the late 19th Century, anti-Semitism became an organised movement with its own political parties.

The Russian Empire had restricted Jews to western regions known as the Pale of Settlement. In 1882, new laws, drafted after widespread anti-Jewish riots, or pogroms, had broken out in the Russian Pale the previous year, stripped Jews of their rural landholdings and restricted them to the towns and cities within the Pale. These measures, which crippled many Jews' activities as rural traders and artisans, spurred the emigration of more than a million Jews to the United States, England and other places over the next four decades.

So anti-Semitism, a virus of hatred that had developed from within the Church, was able to adapt with the times. One good thing is that the Church has finally seen the error of its ways. Even the Catholic Church, the main villains of the piece, have finally admitted their error, officially announcing at Vatican Council II in 1965 that the Jews *"should not be presented as rejected by God or accursed."* Historically, when you look at Church history, as we have done, from the early Church right through to Martin Luther and what was known as the Reformation, one important fact sticks out – the common person was never given a Bible to read! Bible reading and interpretation was in the hands of the leaders and teachers, who had their own agendas to fulfil and used the Bible to justify their own vices, be it lust for money, power, or just good old-fashioned lust!

As soon as the Bible was put in the hands of the masses, people read it and, at the very least, saw no basis for anti-Semitism and at best saw many justifications for a positive attitude towards their Jewish brethren. And this is still the case. Christians today are better informed than "Christians" of yesteryear. Anyone who reads the Bible would have no excuse for reading anti-Semitism into it, unless their judgement is clouded by their own agendas.

So we return to *agendas*. What has really been behind the historical "Christian" attitude towards the Jews? This is a time for truth and self-reflection, because this is no cosy agenda, this is one that, in its ultimate form, resulted in the Holocaust.

God has provided us with the Bible to guide us towards a godly life and to allow us to know His ways. We follow the words of Scripture, are blessed by them, and often are spurred into action by them. Now, it is these actions that are especially significant because it concerns one's views on a whole people, the Jews, and a whole nation, Israel. Is a particular reading of Scripture regarding the Jews a justification for the blind hatred that has been shown by those professing a religion of love and forgiveness, or did the hatred come first?

Arguments against the Jews have been used by such Church luminaries as John Chrysostom, Augustine, Tertullian, Origen, Irenaeus and Martin Luther and many others. It wasn't long before their theology and teachings gave way to practical action in the form of persecution, expulsion and extermination, solely on the basis of the arguments that the Jews had been *replaced* by the Church. Although in our day the Church has laid aside this physical action, the theology that inspired it is still with us. Do you think that God is happy to see His Scriptures interpreted in such a way by leading Christian teachers? I think not.

It is a sad fact that one of the most unifying concepts through Church history has not been theology or the teachings of Jesus, but negativity towards the Jewish people. That is putting it mildly!

Now let's return to the questions posed at the head of this chapter. Do you believe the Jewish people are eternally cursed as a result of their rejection of Jesus? Do you believe they have forfeited their right to be the "chosen people"? Do you believe that Christians have supplanted the Jewish people as the only "people of God"?

If you still truthfully believe in this final statement, ask yourself one fresh question: If God can reject His Old Testament people for their sins, why would a God of justice not reject His New Testament people for committing the very same sins and more? (Any reading of Church history will bear testimony to this.)

So what is your agenda? Your agenda is dictated by your truthful answer to that final question. There is no middle ground and I believe that historians looking back from the future will agree that there was *no more important question* for Christians to answer.

And, finally, to be even more awkward, we will consider the *roots* behind the agendas. For those historically, from Justin Martyr to those who virulently promote replacement theology as a cover for their anti-Semitism, there is only one true root. It may be dressed up as righteous anger or excused as theological research, but it all boils down to a four lettered word: *hate*. This hatred, called *the Longest Hatred* by many, has a spiritual source and for a clear exposition of its origins and purpose I direct you towards my book, *The People of Many Names*. Yes, it's a blatant plug, but I have to be honest that the facts in that book are laid out as clear as they can be and there I rest my case!

It is the summary of that book that marks this out as the *mother of all battles*. I leave you with a short quote from the late Derek Prince, taken from his teaching letter (No. 7) on *The Root of Anti-Semitism*.

While I was preaching in our local church in Jerusalem, quite unexpectedly I heard myself say, "Anti-Semitism can be summed up in one word – MESSIAH!!" At that moment I understood that from its beginning Anti-Semitism had one source – Satan – who was motivated by the knowledge that the One who was to be his conqueror, the Messiah, would come through a people that would be specially prepared by God.

This battle is going to run and run...

Do The Right Thing

Perhaps the most startling, awesome and uncompromising statement that Jesus made was when he was trying to comfort his closest friends. He was speaking of his Father's house with many rooms, which he was going to prepare for them. Thomas was flummoxed because Jesus told them that they knew the way to this house, but Thomas couldn't figure it out. *Lord, we don't know where this place is, so how can we know the way to get there?*

What Jesus said next I am going to analyse in chunks, as his words progressively reveal some wonderful truths.

I am... (hey, isn't he using the words that God used to describe himself to Moses from the burning bush?)... the way... (oh, I get it, he's not giving directions to this house, he *is* the way to the house)... and the truth... (if so, then we must listen to him intently)... and the life... (and we must do what he does).

He is not showing us a roadmap, a set of instructions, a guidebook to find Heaven, or his Father's house. He is not *showing* us the way, he is telling us that he *is* the vehicle, the transportation that's going to get us there. And, more than that, he is not *a* way to Heaven, he is *the* way to Heaven. His next statement makes this abundantly clear.

No one comes to the Father except through me. (John 14:6)

Hey, this is a bit exclusive isn't it? Is Jesus saying that he is the only way to get to Heaven? Apparently so and the reason why he made this claim is wrapped up in a mystery stretching back to the dawn of time, to the moment Adam and Eve ate the forbidden fruit. This is when they set in place the grand sweeping scenario of life in a fallen World, which is still being played out today. You've seen the story, strung together through selected Bible verses, in the tracts that are thrust into your hands at shopping malls (not that this is a bad thing).

Adam and Eve ate the fruit and sinned, creating a gulf between themselves (and all mankind) and God. Mankind was tainted with sin and, because of the very nature of God, there could be no close fellowship any more. From now on the only way to bridge this gap and get right with God was through the shedding of blood. Don't question this, analyse it or doubt it, it's just the way it is. To ensure a good relationship with God one had to cover one's sins with the blood of an animal sacrifice, shed on one's behalf. That's why Adam and Eve were clothed in animal skin (the first sacrifice having been made), Abel's sacrifice of a burnt offering was accepted and Cain's sacrifice of fruit and veg wasn't, and why the whole sacrificial system was developed, from the altars of the Patriarchs, to the tabernacle in the wilderness, to the Temple in Jerusalem. This whole system was developed into a veritable industry, from the rearing of the animals, their inspection for purity and acceptability, the whole mechanism for creating different sacrifices for different purposes and a hierarchical priesthood and associated staff, to musicians and moneychangers, all to keep the thing running.

Then around 30AD the whole thing was done away with, by the sacrifice of Jesus, the Lamb of God, the *atonement*. To push home the point 40 years later, God ensured that the Jews could never return to the old ways, by having the Romans destroy the Jerusalem Temple, thus ensuring that sacrifices could never be made again. According to the writer to the Hebrews, *Jesus has become the guarantee of a better covenant* (Hebrews 7:22). The death of Jesus had done away with the need for any form of animal sacrifice. There is no room here for deep theology; theologians and Christian writers have spent lifetimes covering this subject. It all boils down to this:

> ...*just as the result of one trespass (Adam's) was condemnation for all men, so also the result of one act of righteousness (Jesus's) was justification that brings life for all men.*
> (Romans 5:18)

So Jesus is the way, the *only* way to God, through this act of righteousness, his undeserved death on a cross, a *justification to bring life for all men.*

If this is so, then what does this say about those people who follow other faiths, religions and variations on mainstream Christianity? Is salvation to be found in any other place?

Let us first remind ourselves what Jesus told his friends:

> *Jesus answered, "I am the way and the truth and the life. No one comes to the Father except through me."*
> (John 14:6)

And also the words of Simon Peter:

> *Salvation is found in no one else, for there is no other name under heaven given to men by which we must be saved.*
> (Acts 4:12)

Contrast this with the words of Oprah Winfrey:

> *"Jesus can't possibly be the only way to God..."*
>   (on one of her shows)

So who can we believe? Let's get a historical perspective.

The generation who knew Jesus were quite clear in their beliefs on this matter. There was only one way of pleasing God. It was not about good deeds, sacrifices, prayers, rituals, liturgy, hymns or fasting. These were all ways to a holy life, but the only *way* to God was through faith in the death and resurrection of Jesus Christ, the way, the truth and the life.

Peter declared this to the Jews, in a way they would understand:

Peter replied, "Repent and be baptized, every one of you, in the name of Jesus Christ for the forgiveness of your sins. And you will receive the gift of the Holy Spirit. The promise is for you and your children and for all who are far off—for all whom the Lord our God will call."
(Acts 2:38-39)

And Paul did the same for the Greeks, in a way they would understand:

Therefore since we are God's offspring, we should not think that the divine being is like gold or silver or stone—an image made by man's design and skill. In the past God overlooked such ignorance, but now he commands all people everywhere to repent. For he has set a day when he will judge the world with justice by the man he has appointed. He has given proof of this to all men by raising him from the dead.
(Acts 17:29-31)

But what of the early Church Fathers? It seems that for them, people fell into three different groups: those who believed in Jesus (who were saved), those with heretical beliefs (who were doomed) and the rest (who may be saved). Writing of this latter group, Justin Martyr said that those who live by *reason* were actually "Christians" and those who didn't were wicked men and enemies of Christ. (First Apology 46)

So what had happened to the exclusive certainties of the first Christians? According to Justin, just being able to think and reason seems to have suddenly become the entry requirement for the Kingdom. Now how Greek was that?!

Clement of Alexandria seemed to agree with this:

> *Before the coming of the Lord, philosophy was necessary for justification to the Greeks; now it is useful for piety . . . for it brought the Greeks to Christ as the law did the Hebrews.*
>
> (Miscellanies 1:5)

Origen went even further to broaden the entry requirements. He proposed something called universal salvation or *universalism*, which is sure to get the discernment radar tingling. The idea behind this is that, since God is love, everyone (including Satan) will find salvation, even if this is after death, and the whole creation would return to a state of pure spirit.

This is pure Platonism, the idea of the soul being trapped in our body and longing to complete the cycle by returning to God, from where it came in the first place. This idea diminishes our life on Earth, viewing it just as a passing stage in a great journey, rather than the Biblical view which states that what happens to us on Earth is *vitally* important.

> *Just as man is destined to die once, and after that to face judgment.*
> (Hebrews 9:27)

What of Augustine, the key man for the medieval Church? For a start he rejected universalism, placing an emphasis on original sin, the separation of man and God and the need for reconciliation. As we have already seen, Augustine was followed by a period of increasing domination of the individual believer by the structures, liturgies and instructions of the State Church.

Extra Ecclesiam nulla salus. A Latin phrase that summed up the beliefs of the early Catholic Church. It translates as "outside the Church there is no salvation". This didn't actually mean that everyone who attended Church was saved, in fact Augustine himself said, "how many sheep there are without, how many wolves within"!

But how were people saved within the Catholic Church? Was it just through a simple belief in the redemptive work of Jesus Christ? Yes... and no. It was considered the first step, but there was another step to make as well. These were the sacraments – baptism, penance, eucharist, confirmation, matrimony, holy orders and anointing of the sick – supposedly *the vehicles of his grace.* These seven sacraments were said to be necessary for salvation and as most of them had to be administered by an authorised person from *within* the Church, then you can see how the Latin phrase was enforced. This was why many Churches of that period were built with the baptismal font near the entrance. It was a nudge to the subconscious mind that the entrance to Heaven was to be paralleled through baptism, the first sacrament of the Church.

So, whereas the Church of the apostles emphasised belief in Jesus as the necessary and sufficient means of salvation, the Church that followed (of the early Church Fathers) implied that this was no longer necessary and the Catholic Church that followed implied that it was no longer sufficient. Universalism followed by exclusivism! What a tangled web was weaved!

We now turn to Thomas Aquinas. He seemed to agree with Augustine on the issue of salvation.

Since, however, the death of Christ is, so to say, the universal cause of human salvation, and since a universal cause must be applied singly to each of its effects, it was necessary to show men some remedies through which the benefit of Christ's death could somehow be conjoined to them. It is of this sort, of course, that the sacraments of the Church are said to be.

(Summa contra Gentiles 4:56)

The sacraments were, and still are, very much part of the Catholic solution for maintaining good relations with the Creator. One would expect this to not be the case when Martin Luther and the Protestants arrived on the scene.

So at last came the Reformers with their open Bibles and their *solas*. *Sola fide*, by faith alone, through grace alone in Christ alone. We seem to be back where we started off, a simple faith in the completed work of Jesus Christ, through dying on the cross for our sins.

> *For it is by grace you have been saved, through faith and this not from yourselves, it is the gift of God not by works, so that no one can boast.*
> (Ephesians 2:8-9)

Every Christian era has its own problems, usually brought about by too much analytical Greek thinking. The Reformers, trained and educated, thinking men of their day, liked a good argument, just like the Church Fathers and the Ancient Greeks, their ancestral equivalents. Have you heard of Occam's razor (the simplest solution is usually the best one)? Well, you can throw that out of the window for a start, as the Protestants took simple basic Biblical truths... and analysed them.

Out of this great ruminatory rigmarole came the following conclusions, beliefs and schools of thought concerning the mechanism of salvation, the *atonement*. One historical viewpoint is the *satisfaction* view of the atonement, acceptable to both the Catholics and the Lutherans. Then there is the *substitution* view, favoured by the Calvinists, also the *moral* influence view, the *governmental* view and the *limited* view of the atonement. Then there is the *ransom* view, favoured by some in the Word of Faith movement. Please don't interpret a lack of systematic comparison of these theologies as a lack of respect of the importance of these issues. I really don't want to steer you into the stormy waters of *Calvinism vs Arminianism, Free Will vs Predestination, Once*

Saved Always Saved? or any other theological joust, otherwise we will surely lose ourselves. It is simply to make the point of how easy it is for a simple faith to suffer at the altar of over-analysis.

Although the Reformation was not a complete one and resulted in a plethora of state Churches throughout Europe, it did mostly bring the focus back to personal salvation, rather than through the sacraments. One effect of the plethora of views was that Christians began to think deeper about who was going to receive salvation and whether faith in the death and resurrection of Jesus Christ was the only way. John Calvin, one of the key Reformers, was certain of this belief and spoke quite strongly against those, such as fellow Reformer Zwingli, who disagreed. Calvin wrote:

> *All the more vile is the stupidity of those people who open heaven to all the impious and unbelieving, without the grace of him whom Scripture teaches to be the only door by which we enter into salvation.*

Yet, the certainties shared by Calvin and those who preceded him were beginning to slowly crumble as the World around them started to change at an increasing pace, with the rise of rationalism and the scientific age. The World was opening up. Explosions in the growth of transportation and communications were allowing for new freedoms in human interactions. For some this was a foretaste of Heaven, for others this brought uncertainties and confusion.

Christians were becoming exposed to folk of other denominations, who held most things in common with them, but not everything. Others, who would have once been condemned or even killed as heretics, were living freely and debating their positions. Still others had left behind any semblance of Christian belief but were living virtuous lives, either as followers of some humanistic creed or just as good, honest, up-standing citizens. Then there were those who followed other gods, the Mohammedans, Hindus and Buddhists. And those pesky Jews were still around!

Jesus answered, "I am the way and the truth and the life. No one comes to the Father except through me."
(John 14:6)

Salvation is found in no one else, for there is no other name under heaven given to men by which we must be saved.
(Acts 4:12)

And this is the testimony: God has given us eternal life, and this life is in his Son. He who has the Son has life; he who does not have the Son of God does not have life.
(1 John 5:11-12)

It was easy to believe in this if you only knew like-minded Christians, who believed as you did. What about the others? Yes there were those unrepentant non-believers who didn't *deserve* salvation – the liars, cheats, murderers, adulterers, blasphemers, drunks and vagabonds – but what of the others?

According to a survey of American Christians in 2008 (Pew Forum on Religion and Public Life) 52% of them believed that non-Christian faiths *had the power to save individuals*. Of these people, around a quarter of them even felt that atheists could get to Heaven!

This is a serious statistic. This is declaring that salvation could be achieved through other gods or even through no god at all. Where do these ideas come from? Is it from Scripture or is it from the World?

Can it be from Scripture? It is always possible to find Scriptures to support any position you would want to take if you look hard enough. I mentioned this in an earlier chapter, it is called *eisegesis*. People have been doing this since near the beginning of the Church Age and have used God's Word to justify anything from what to eat to who to kill! But God does not look kindly on those who mangle His words; that's not why He put them there. God's words are there to illuminate minds and convict hearts. For instance,

Charles Manson, the mass-murderer, saw himself as the fifth angel of Revelation 9:1, plainly a distortion brought forth from a disturbed mind.

Now people are always going to find verses in the Bible that seem to indicate salvation other than through faith in Jesus Christ.

> ... that we have put our hope in the living God, who is the Savior of all men, and especially of those who believe.
> (1 Timothy 4:10)

> For as in Adam all die, so in Christ all will be made alive.
> (1 Corinthians 15:22)

> ... and through him to reconcile to himself all things, whether things on earth or things in heaven, by making peace through his blood, shed on the cross.
> (Colossians 1:20)

> Consequently, just as the result of one trespass was condemnation for all men, so also the result of one act of righteousness was justification that brings life for all men.
> (Romans 5:18)

Each of these have been used by *universalists* (yes, they are still around) to assert that all human beings will be saved and enjoy everlasting life with Jesus Christ. Yet each of these verses in the hand of a proper theologian can be explained away to mean something entirely different.

And this brings me back to:

> Jesus answered, "I am the way and the truth and the life. No one comes to the Father except through me."
> (John 14:6)

This can't be explained away. I haven't found a credible commentator who views this verse in any way other than the plain meaning of the words.

Which means that there is only one unavoidable, uncomfortable, perhaps painful, conclusion.

Faith in the death and resurrection of Jesus Christ is the only way to heaven. There it is.

So what do we say to the universalists, or the Catholics who insist on the sacraments, or those who follow another Jesus or other gods or no gods? Are they all wrong? If so, who are we to correct them, because some of them are seriously clever people? Are they all doomed? If so, who are we to condemn them, because some of them are seriously good people?

Before we consider this, let us consider ourselves.

So we return to *agendas*. If you passionately disagree with my argument so far in this chapter then there's probably one word that comes to mind: *intolerance*.

The general thinking today is that, in these days of multi-culturalism, with folk of many faiths and no faiths sharing the global village, we Christians must be more inclusive and show more tolerance to others.

What should our reaction to this be?

What's more important, tolerance or truth? We can engage with the World in a spirit of tolerance, accepting other viewpoints, making concessions and handing over ground. We can do this to make people happy and make us feel good, but there's a sacrifice involved. We can conjure up a version of the gospel, that promises fluffiness, comfort and cosiness, that convinces us that the God of love is going to welcome everyone into Heaven with a great big smile in his beaming bearded old face.

Or we can live by the words of Jesus:

Jesus answered, "I am the way and the truth and the life. No one comes to the Father except through me".
(John 14:6)

This uncompromising unforgiving certainty may be at odds with your picture of God. Who do you worship; a sentimental Santa-like caricature that has been fed to us by the media – Christian or otherwise – or the real God of holiness and righteousness, who is incapable of sharing Heaven, by His very nature, with men and women who have not seriously dealt with their sins?

Tolerance or truth? Which is your agenda?

If tolerance is your agenda, then we must also consider the root of this agenda. What motivates your tolerance? Perhaps you would say a sense of fair play, even love. Humanly speaking, who could disagree with that? What could be better than people getting along with each other? After all, how many have been killed through the evils of intolerance, particularly religious intolerance? Wasn't 9/11 a product of this very evil?

But we are not speaking … *humanly*. We are put on this Earth to act… *biblically*.

Jesus answered, "I am the way and the truth and the life. No one comes to the Father except through me."
(John 14:6)

At the end of the day it is truth, not tolerance, that is going to get people into Heaven. And the rest… ? We'll read about the alternative in the next chapter.

That Horrible Doctrine

We've discussed the crime, now it's time for the punishment. Or, to put it another way, where is it that the Bible says we are all heading… unless drastic action is taken? This chapter is not so much about the crime or the journey, but it's *all* about the destination.

Hell. Is it real and, if so, what's it like? After all, it is a horrible word, used as an all purpose negative term. Hell's kitchen, Hell's teeth, Hell's bells, Hell on Earth. It's the most horrible doctrine of them all, which is why we hear little of it in church. It's the rotten festering corpse of the elephant in the room of the Christian faith. It's the un-mentionable, unspeakable and embarrassing doctrine. It's been used to scare people into the Kingdom, but has just as often scared people away, because of its apparently irrational awfulness.

All that we need to know about Hell is to read the words of the one who spoke most about it, Jesus himself. In fact, Jesus spoke more of Hell than he did of Heaven. He spoke of it over 40 times in the book of Matthew alone! A sobering thought. Just using the actual words from his mouth, recorded by Matthew, here are some of these:

Hell is… a place of fire (Matthew 5:22).
Hell is… a place where your whole body is cast into (Matthew 5:29, 30).

Hell is... a place of darkness (Matthew 8:12)
Hell is... a place of weeping (Matthew 8:12)
Hell is... a place of gnashing of teeth (Matthew 8:12)
Hell is... a place of torture (Matthew 8:29)
Hell is... a place of eternal punishment (Matthew 25:46)

Jesus is being very specific, very direct. This is not gentle Jesus, meek and mild, this is not baby Jesus nursing at his mother's breast, this is not the loving Jesus who opens Heaven to all. This is not a popular picture of Jesus, there is not a trace of sugar-coating here. To many Christians, a Jesus who condemns to Hell all who don't believe in him, is unacceptable. We remind ourselves of the verse:

> *Jesus answered, "I am the way and the truth and the life. No one comes to the Father except through me."*
> (John 14:6)

Jesus is saying here quite clearly that those who reject him *don't* come to the Father but end up in a dark place of eternal punishment, where all can be heard is weeping and gnashing of teeth. This is presumably where you'd find Hitler and Stalin. No problems there. It's also where you'd find your favourite auntie Jean, who never had a bad word to say against anyone and who was kindness personified, but was an atheist to her dying breath. She'd be there in utter darkness for eternity weeping and gnashing her teeth. It's a soul-wrenching thought, because we all have auntie Jeans and the mental picture of these virtuous people in such a place is just awesomely horrible. What was Jesus thinking of?

Do we voice the thoughts of the atheist thinker Bertrand Russell, who said, "anyone who threatens someone with eternal punishment is inhumane"? Surely every ounce of your humanity would agree with this and would add the assertion that a *God of love* could never act in this way.

Do we voice the thoughts of many Christians who take refuge in their belief that Jesus' stark descriptions of Hell are just symbolic language, meant to convey the idea that Hell is a rather nasty place to end up without expecting his listeners to take him at face value? I challenge you just to read the verses at the head of the chapter and decide whether you are reading a literal account or just symbolism. If you prefer symbolism then you are simply following in the footsteps of Philo, Origen and the allegorists, who trawled through Scripture and simply declared that anything that didn't fit in with their agenda had deeper spiritual meanings rather than any face value meaning.

Perhaps at this point a historical perspective would be useful to us to see how the concept of Hell has developed since Jesus' time.

We start with the Church Fathers and are perhaps surprised to discover that their views on Hell are much the same as Jesus' views.

Justin Martyr

We have been taught that only they may aim at immortality who have lived a holy and virtuous life near to God. We believe that they who live wickedly and do not repent will be punished in everlasting fire.

("First Apology" 21)

Irenaeus

The penalty increases for those who do not believe the Word of God and despise his coming. . . . [I]t is not merely temporal, but eternal. To whomsoever the Lord shall say, 'Depart from me, accursed ones, into the everlasting fire,' they will be damned forever.

("Against Heresies" 4:28:2)

Tertullian

After the present age is ended he will judge his worshipers for a reward of eternal life and the godless for a fire equally perpetual and unending.

("Apology" 18:3)

What of the troublesome Origen? As we discovered in the last chapter, here things start to change. To recap, he proposed universal salvation or *universalism*, which said that, since God is love, everyone (including Satan) will find salvation, even if this is after death, and the whole Creation would return to a state of pure spirit. So, for this Christian philosopher, God's love will triumph and none will go to Hell.

Where did he get these strange ideas from? It is down to the way that he viewed the ability of people to make decisions, the concept of *free will*. The usual Christian view is that we all have the capacity to either accept or reject God and our eternal destination depends on that decision. But Origen was heavily influenced by Plato who stated that free will was not a case of choosing between good and evil, but merely doing the best one could according to how educated or mature you were. For him there was no such thing as evil, so people never *chose* to do evil things, they were simply acting out of ignorance. So our soul would be continually re-born in different bodies until it lost this ignorance, learnt to do good all the time and achieved salvation! It sounds a bit like re-incarnation except that, in Plato's system, there was no chance of ending up as a goldfish or an elephant. But Christian it certainly was not!

We move on to Augustine, the Catholic touchstone. He certainly believed in Hell, which is not surprising as he was the theological founder of Western Christianity, who introduced systematic teaching on original sin, the fall and predestination. His view on infants was interesting and revealing and was a result of disagreements he was having with an English gentleman known as Pelagius.

Pelagius denied original sin, inasmuch as Adam merely set a "bad example" for us, contrasting with Jesus' "good example" thousands of years later. Each of us therefore had perfect free will to choose between good and evil, without the taint of a sinful nature or the need of the grace of God. Regarding the death of those too young to have had a chance to consciously sin, Pelagius said that the infant would not go to Hell, but to another nicer place, usually known as *Limbo*. Augustine differed in this and emphasised the need for infant baptism, to ensure a passage to Heaven, otherwise the infant was going directly to Hell, albeit to a milder punishment than an adult would experience.

Augustine even thought he knew where Hell was, *under the Earth*. He's not alone in this thinking, after all it is also known as the *underworld*. As we move into the medieval period, through the superstition of the Dark Ages and the subsequent ecclesiastical control of the Catholic Church, Hell becomes a place much discussed by the chattering classes, as well as the great unwashed of the day. The medieval equivalent of J. K. Rowling, John Grisham and their ilk was an epic poem by the Italian, Dante Alighieri. It was the *Divine Comedy*, the first part of which was titled *Inferno*, the Italian word for "Hell".

In Inferno, Hell becomes nine circles of suffering, entered by Dante and his guide, the Roman poet, Virgil. They enter on Good Friday, on a search for God and exit on Easter Sunday. These nine circles are inhabited by those being punished for various sins, including the lustful, the gluttonous, hoarders, the wrathful, heretics, the violent, frauds and traitors. Each sinner is punished in an ironic fashion, for instance fortune-tellers have their heads on back to front, unable to see what is in front of them! As they progress, the severity of the sins increase and the circles get smaller, until, at the centre of the Earth, they find Satan himself.

Of course none of this is from the Bible; it is allegory. For Dante, Hell was populated by famous people from his day and earlier, including many from the Church, including Pope Anastasius II (heretic) and Andrea de' Mozzi (bishop and sodomite). Interestingly, the first circle visited is Limbo, inhabited by those who died before Jesus lived, where he meets, among others, Aristotle and Plato.

Dante's poem has made a huge impact right to the present day, interpreted for a less literate generation, through the mediums of movies and computer games. T.S. Eliot, the 20th Century poet, claimed that *Dante and Shakespeare divide the modern World between them!* Inferno is said to have inspired the movie versions of The Lord of the Rings. Others have even said that without Dante there would be no Twilight Zone, Close Encounters of the Third Kind or E.T.! Work that one out for yourself (it's beyond me!)

So perhaps, for subsequent generations, the landscape of Hell owes more to this work of fiction than it does to the sparse narrative provided by the Bible. Now, I wonder what the Protestant Reformers thought...?

The definitive statement is taken from the Westminster Confession, dating from 1646.

> ... but the wicked, who know not God, and obey not the
> gospel of Jesus Christ, shall be cast into eternal torments,
> and punished with everlasting destruction from the presence
> of the Lord, and from the glory of his power.
>
> (Chapter XXXIII, Of the Last Judgment)

In other words, it's a straight-forward Biblical understanding. Jesus would have concurred. Remember, the Reformers believed in *Sola Scriptura*, Scripture alone, and, as uncomfortable it may be to say so, Jesus' thoughts on the reality of Hell are clear and unambiguous. Any deviation from this Sola Scriptura approach to the understanding of the doctrine of Hell will not come from anything that the Bible has to say about the subject, but rather what subsequent commentators have to say about the truth of the Bible and the character of God.

The Age of Enlightenment and the rise of humanism, as you would expect, brought about vast changes in the perception of such matters. Being a movement that put man at the centre of everything and relegating God to the sidelines at best, the idea of Hell would be the first Christian doctrine jettisoned. And so it was. Therefore it wasn't an issue for anyone other than mainstream Christians and the fringe cults.

But this is not to say that Christians in modern times have been in agreement as to what exactly happens in Hell. Far from it. Variations on the theme have given us a Hell that has many faces, depending on what tradition you follow. Let us see...

We start with the Roman Catholics.

To die in mortal sin without repenting and accepting God's merciful love means remaining separated from him for ever by our own free choice. This state of definitive self- exclusion from communion with God and the blessed is called "Hell".

(Catechism of the Catholic Church)

This may be vaguely religious but only a half truth. Yes, Hell is a place of separation from God, *but what about the punishment?*

Pope John Paul II seems to have stepped even further back from what the Bible says, when he said, *the images of Hell that Sacred Scripture presents to us must be correctly interpreted. They show the complete frustration and emptiness of life without God. Rather than a place, Hell indicates the state of those who freely and definitively separate themselves from God, the source of all life and joy.*

Rather than a place? Interestingly, his successor, Pope Benedict XVI seems to have got the Catholics back on track, if an article in The Times in March 2007 is to be believed, reporting on a meeting in Rome:

Hell is a place where sinners really do burn in an everlasting fire, and not just a religious symbol designed to galvanise the faithful, the Pope has said... Hell "really exists and is eternal, even if nobody talks about it much any more",
he said.

The Vatican seemed embarrassed by this. A Church historian Agostino Paravicini Bagliani gave a glimpse of the party line. He stated that the concept of Hell had been misused in the Middle Ages to scare the flock. He also said,

"The problem is not only that our sense of sin has declined, but also that the world wars and totalitarianisms of the 20th Century created a Hell on Earth as bad as anything we can imagine in the afterlife."

Jesus gave us a perfectly good idea of Hell, a place of total darkness where one undergoes severe discomfort for eternity. No *Hell on Earth* is ever going to compare with this!

So who do we go with, the infallible pope or the Catholic spin-doctors? As the latter represent official Catholic policy we can make the following conclusion about their view on the doctrine of Hell.

Let's scare the flock a little bit but there's no point terrifying them too much, or we'll start losing more of them.

I decided to have a brief look at the main UK Protestant denominations, by visiting the main website of each and reading their doctrinal statements. What I found was interesting, disturbing and probably worth examining in another book. Every website was designed to appeal to the eye, to show social relevance and cultural insights. But what these people actually believe – the original raison d'être of the denominations after all – was either very well hidden or totally missing. I found no doctrinal statements for the Church of England or the Methodists and, if I wanted to know more about what the Baptists believe, I would need to post them a cheque for £14.50 for their full constitution!

If I can't access this information as someone with professional experience of working with websites, then how is the general public meant to find what should be basic and freely available information?

Why is it so hard to find out what today's denominations actually believe? Is it because *some doctrines* are in our politically-correct, spiritually-correct and ecumenical age too divisive or even undefendable for them?

So, as the front doors were locked, I went through the back door.

For the Baptists, I went to the American equivalent, the Southern Baptists. Their website was frankly not very visually stimulating, but I was able to get a full statement of beliefs with one mouse click. I was also able to easily view a whole batch of sermons on the subject of Hell. The sermons were all good and biblical, although the official statement of faith was a bit sparse.

The unrighteous will be consigned to Hell, the place of everlasting punishment.

As for the Methodists, John Wesley, their founder, certainly did believe in a literal Biblical Hell. He wrote a sermon, "Of Hell" that was crystal clear on the subject.

As for our pains on earth, blessed be God, they are not eternal. There are some intervals to relieve and there is some period to finish them. When we ask a friend that is sick, how he does; 'I am in pain now,' says he, 'but I hope to be easy soon.' This is a sweet mitigation of the present uneasiness. But how dreadful would his case be if he should answer, 'I am all over pain, and I shall never be eased of it. I lie under exquisite torment of body, and horror of soul; and I shall feel it for ever!' Such is the case of the damned sinners in hell. Suffer any pain, then, rather than come into that place of torment!

But what of today's Methodists? Again I had to go to the American website, that of the United Methodist Church. I needed three mouse clicks to get to their "basic affirmations" only to discover that statements on Heaven and Hell were missing and I would need to buy a book to find out more.

Now for the good old Church of England. The closest I could get to a firm opinion from the Anglicans was a 1995 report from their Doctrine Commission, entitled "The Mystery of Salvation". It was a 225 page report, but only one page hit the headlines – the part of the report where Hell was examined. Here's what they said:

"Hell is not eternal torment, but it is the final and irrevocable choosing of that which is opposed to God so completely and so absolutely that the only end is total non-being." [p.199]

Oh dear. I will comment on this a little later.

Two more denominations, the Pentecostals, who seem to revert to a more Biblical understanding:

We believe in the bodily resurrection of all men, the everlasting conscious bliss of all who truly believe in our Lord Jesus Christ and the everlasting conscious punishment of all whose names are not written in the Book of Life.

(Assemblies of God)

THE FUTURE STATE: *We believe in the resurrection of the dead and in the final judgement of the world, the eternal conscious bliss of the righteous and the eternal conscious punishment of the wicked.* (Elim)

Now for the leading Evangelical organisation in the UK, the Evangelical Alliance. They produced a report in 2000 entitled, "The Nature of Hell". It was not an unsubstantial document and it had 22 conclusions. Here's the thrust of their argument:

◊ Hell is separation from God.

◊ Hell involves severe punishment, though Scripture used is often metaphorical.

◊ Hell is a conscious experience of rejection and torment.

◊ Hell involves degrees of punishment and suffering in hell related to the severity of sins committed on Earth.

◊ Hell is a realm of destruction, which could be of actual existence of individual sinners or to the quality of their relationship with God.

◊ Hell is eternal though not necessarily as a ceaseless conscious experience.

◊ Hell can involve conditional immortality (more of that later).

Before we unravel this doctrinal ball of yarn it is worth noting the opening two statements of their report:

In the contemporary interpretation of Scriptural teaching
on Hell, as on other doctrines, we look to the Holy Spirit to
illuminate us and lead us into the truth.

This seems to be a cop out, in that it implies that there is something special about contemporary society that the Holy Spirit feels the need to re-evaluate interpretations of Hell that have served the Church well for 2000 years.

In reflecting on the doctrine of Hell, we look for practical application to the church's urgent task of mission and evangelism.

Truth is truth, regardless of its practical applications. Is compromise to be acceptable if it pulls in more people to the Kingdom?

The problem for the writers of this report is their need to accommodate the various views in the broad sweep of evangelicalism. They recognise that *the interpretation of Hell as eternal conscious punishment is the one most widely attested by the Church in its historic formulation of doctrine and in its understanding of Scripture.*

But this is no longer the dominant evangelical position these days, neither is it the dominant position in the wider Christian community. For a start there is the *universalism* of Origen, as introduced in the last chapter. These are the people who believe that a God of love doesn't want anyone to end up in Hell and that everyone will be saved. There are some who still take this position, or a variation on it, but they are not a significant number.

Then we have the current position of the Catholics and most evangelicals today and that is a Hell with the heat turned down, just a hint of darkness and a bit of discomfort (unless you've been particularly rotten). This is a Hell palatable for modern man, an acceptable Hell that the evangelists can work with, a Hell that doesn't embarrass our view of a loving God who wouldn't hurt a flea, a Hell that doesn't bracket you with medieval superstitions or, even worse, the *fundamentalists!*

It's a Hell that you can sell to potential converts, to convince them that today's Church is made up of nice people worshipping a nice God, not one who is going to condemn all non-believers to eternal conscious torture. It's a very British Hell. It's a Hell where you are separate from God (which is correct) and where you are free to contemplate how bad you've been.

Others of the same sensibilities take a different approach. It's a "gone in a puff of smoke" type of Hell, *annihilationism*. This is the party line of the Church of England and of many evangelicals, including, as I am told, John Stott, John Wenham and Roger Forster. In this scheme people are utterly destroyed at some point after death and judgement. They just cease to be, no eternity in Heaven or Hell. Similar to this is the idea of *conditional immortality* which states that only the saved have eternal lives, presumably making it easier to annihilate the wicked! Annihilationism is also believed by fringe Christian groups/cults such as the Jehovah's Witnesses and Christadelphians.

So that's where we are with *this horrible doctrine*. The traditional position believed by Jesus, the apostles, the early Church Fathers, Augustine and the medieval Catholics, the Reformers and today's *"fundamentalists"* (though I would prefer to call them "Biblical Christians"), is in decline. It is not because God has changed His mind or that Christians have misinterpreted the words of Jesus, but rather that the World has moved on. Nowadays Christians do not rely solely on the Bible for doctrinal instruction; instead other factors from outside are brought to bear, never more apparent than in the case of the doctrine of Hell. This brings me to the recurring theme of agendas. What agenda is followed by those who follow a particular interpretation of the doctrine?

Again the default agenda for those who take the traditional position of Hell as eternal conscious punishment is the desire for *Sola Scriptura*, for the Bible alone to inform your opinion. For the Christian who has sincere concern for the lost and just cannot fathom the thought of such a fierce fate for unbelievers their agenda may seem to be compassion, but it is mixed with denial. It's a

Christian sentimentalism, that is happy to go along with the nice doctrines but wishes the bad ones would just go away. As C.S. Lewis once said:

> *There is no doctrine I would more willingly remove from*
> *Christianity than [Hell], if it lay in my power... I would pay*
> *any price to be able to say truthfully: "All will be saved."*
> (The Problem of Pain (London: Geoffrey Bles, 1940), p. 94.)

And what about the root of this sentimentalism? It's not real love because it is not based on Biblical truth. As Hell is the default destination of all humanity because of our sin nature, Jesus' promise of Heaven through faith in his death and resurrection is our only escape from this fate. Any sugar-coating of this fate just serves to minimise the importance for the salvation provided by Jesus. Some people (albeit jokingly) insist they would be quite happy for an after-life separated from God as they have managed to live their lives in the same state. Others insist that annihilation holds no fear for them, as they wouldn't be around to think about it. Yet if the real truth of Hell was *still* preached by all Christians, the fear of Hell would become significant. Not that we should scare people into Heaven, but we should always give people the truth, the whole truth and nothing but the truth.

In the 19th Century, the infamous murderer, Charlie Peace, on the way to his execution, noticed that the prison chaplain had been reading some Bible verses about Hell. Peace remarked, "*if I believed what you and the church of God say that you believe, even if England were covered with broken glass from coast to coast, I would walk over it, if need be, on hands and knees and think it worthwhile living, just to save one soul from an eternal hell like that!*"

One thing still troubles me about this whole matter. This concerns myself, but perhaps you too. Given that we are to believe the words of Jesus in this horrible eternal punishment for the auntie Jeans of this World, shouldn't this provoke in us an insistent relentless heart-felt desire for evangelism? Wouldn't the saving of souls become our highest priority in life? I have searched my soul and, to be perfectly honest, I do not find this passion to any higher degree than the occasional prayer for the specific lost and some half-hearted and clumsy attempts at evangelism. Can't we see where these people are going? Why aren't we doing more about it?

Is it the usual cop-out of *there are others out there who have specific giftings to do the intercession and the evangelism?* Or have we taken on unconscious heretical ideas that our families and loved ones are saved by proxy because of our own beliefs? Or, even worse, perhaps our deepest thoughts have been more affected by the prevailing current Christian worldview than we would care to admit. Perhaps we have, at our deepest level, taken onboard universalism or annihilationism as safer, less problematic options and we are just paying lip-service to the Biblical position?

This worries me. It should worry us all. What worries me *even more* is when this *doesn't* worry me! We ought to be worried.

Let's pray that God can save us from unbelief and error and provoke us to a fresh passion and concern for those who surround us travelling on the road to Hell.

Come Lord Jesus... Already!

A battleground of battlegrounds. These are battles fought with passion by those with firm unshakeable views. Yet most Christians are absent from the conflict, wary of the minefields surrounding the battle. There's passion, there's controversy and there's apathy in equal proportions. Some Christians dedicate their whole ministry to their study of End Times, others avoid it like the plague. The Book of Revelation, the chief source book on the subject, is the favourite Bible book for non-believers but the least read by Christians. Why?

Yes, it's the least read book of the Bible by Christians, yet the only book that has an in-built blessing for its readers.

Blessed is the one who reads the words of this prophecy, and blessed are those who hear it and take to heart what is written in it, because the time is near.
(Revelation 1:3)

Out of all the books of the Bible it's the most mangled by Christians, yet the only book that has an in-built curse for its manglers.

I warn everyone who hears the words of the prophecy of this book: If anyone adds anything to them, God will add to him the

plagues described in this book. And if anyone takes words away
from this book of prophecy, God will take away from him his
share in the tree of life and in the holy city, which are described
in this book.
(Revelation 22:18-19)

It's because of the mangling that folk are not reading it. It's a book
with a lot of baggage attached, it's a book that seems to inhabit the
grey area of symbols and events, where it's unclear which is *symbol*
and which is *event.*

Rather than add to the confusion I am going to demonstrate the
sources of the confusion and, as with our other battlegrounds, we
are going to travel back in time and follow the battle as it rages
through the pages of Church history.

Jesus spoke of a colossal future event in Luke 21:

"When you see Jerusalem being surrounded by armies, you
will know that its desolation is near. Then let those who are
in Judea flee to the mountains, let those in the city get out,
and let those in the country not enter the city. For this is the
time of punishment in fulfillment of all that has been written.
How dreadful it will be in those days for pregnant women
and nursing mothers! There will be great distress in the land
and wrath against this people. They will fall by the sword and
will be taken as prisoners to all the nations. Jerusalem will
be trampled on by the Gentiles until the times of the Gentiles
are fulfilled."
(Luke 21:20-24)

A few decades later this prophecy was to save a significant
proportion of the Jewish Christians living in Jerusalem.

The Romans were approaching to sack the city of Jerusalem
and these believers decided that this was the time that Jesus spoke
about. So they fled to the town of Pella to the east and were saved.
The rest were, as predicted, either killed or captured, ending up

as slaves sent to many nations. And Jerusalem was truly trampled on by the Gentile Romans until... well, that's become a debating point , because the times of the Gentiles, stretching from that point of time into the future, are either fulfilled already or are yet to be fulfilled – depending on your viewpoint.

So Jesus prophesied an event and it was fulfilled and heeded. That seems clear cut. The verses that follow are not so clear cut.

There will be signs in the sun, moon and stars. On the earth, nations will be in anguish and perplexity at the roaring and tossing of the sea. Men will faint from terror, apprehensive of what is coming on the world, for the heavenly bodies will be shaken. At that time they will see the Son of Man coming in a cloud with power and great glory. When these things begin to take place, stand up and lift up your heads, because your redemption is drawing near.
(Luke 21:25-28)

Did this happen, is it going to happen, or is the language used just symbolic or figurative? Let us start our historical journey with the Church Fathers.

Justin Martyr, as the name implies, was killed for his faith. He lived in a time of intense persecution. All the woes that he read from the available Scripture led him to believe that he was living in the End Times and you can't fault him for that.

Irenaeus thought this too and wrote about it in *Against Heresies*, producing a detailed analysis of the Book of Daniel and Revelation, particularly regarding the timetable, activities and identity of the antichrist. He was also the first to muse on "666", however he reached no firm conclusions. He also believed in the literal Millennium Kingdom, the 1000 year reign of Christ and his Church on Earth after the Second Coming.

He was one of the first *premillenialists*. This is the belief that Christ will return *before* the 1000 year Millennium reign of Revelation 20.

I saw thrones on which were seated those who had been given
authority to judge. And I saw the souls of those who had been
beheaded because of their testimony for Jesus and because of
the word of God. They had not worshiped the beast or his image
and had not received his mark on their foreheads or their hands.
They came to life and reigned with Christ a thousand years.
(Revelation 20:4)

This position was strongly opposed by – guess who? – yes it's that
man Origen again. A literal 1000 year reign that the Scriptures
imply was totally unacceptable to this Christian philosopher, the
main promoter of the philosophic ideas of Plato, including the use
of allegory to spiritualise Holy Scripture. The prevailing Greek
worldview was the thought of everything going on forever in a
cyclical sense, with life followed by death, then by life, then by
death and so on, also the idea of the End Time scenario of the
premillenialists was alien to them, and to Origen.

Origen was one of the first *amillenialists*, the belief that there
will be *no* literal 1000 year Millennium reign, but rather that the
1000 years is to be taken *symbolically* and that the Millennium has
actually begun and is the current Church age. A curious implication
of this belief is that Satan is currently bound (Revelation 20:2) and
powerless, which seems to be contrary to popular Christian opinion
and experience!

This all sounds like Origen; the word "symbolically" is the
big give-away, plus his reluctance to accept the plain meaning of
Biblical texts and to relentlessly spiritualise away as much as he
could, in the true spirit of Platonism.

This was also the view of the enormously influential Augustine,
which basically meant that amillennialism became the official
Catholic view at that time, and has remained so ever since. There
were also political reasons, as the Catholic State Church was not
too happy to promote a worldview that involved Christ returning
to do away with the evil rulers of the World! Also, amillennialism
fitted in seamlessly with his whole theological system, regarding

his view of sin, grace and the sacraments, as well as his thoughts on Israel. One thing that he couldn't countenance was a physical 1000 year Kingdom of God on Earth. Plato would never have allowed this.

Although amillennialism remained the dominant position for a long time afterwards, there were a few apocalyptic blips, mainly around the days leading up to the years AD 500 and AD 1000. Then there was the monk, Joachim of Fiore, a fervent premillenialist, who decided that the year AD 1260 was to usher in the Millennium reign of Christ, but died well before his life's work was shown to be nonsense.

We would expect the Reformers to buck the trend. Surely *Sola Scriptura* was going to suggest a literal interpretation of Revelation 20 and a return to premillennialism? Wrong! Martin Luther, John Calvin and the theologians of the Anglican Church felt they had no reason to go against Augustine and his amillennialism.

Martin Luther had very negative feelings about the Book of Revelation and stated in his Preface to the book that *"it makes me consider it to be neither apostolic nor prophetic. Christ is neither taught nor known in it"* (although he eventually changed his mind and rewrote his Preface). It was also the only Bible book that John Calvin didn't write a commentary for. This is very curious, particularly in the light of the verse near the head of this chapter:

> *Blessed is the one who reads the words of this prophecy, and blessed are those who hear it and take to heart what is written in it, because the time is near.*
> (Revelation 1:3)

What was going on here with the Reformers? Were other forces at work here? Why did they so readily continue with many of the views of Augustine, such as amillennialism, which were so blatantly influenced by pagan philosophy? John Calvin was so negative about premillennialists, that he wrote the following:

*Now their fiction is too childish either to need or to be worth
a refutation.*

(Institutes, 3. 25. 5)

As a result of these opinions, the major Protestant denominations
rejected premillennialism. But read on ...

The Lutherans, in the Augsburg Confession of Faith in
1530, state:

*They condemn also others who are now spreading certain
Jewish Opinions, that before the resurrection of the dead the
godly shall take possession of the kingdom of the world, the
ungodly being everywhere suppressed.*

(Article XVII)

The Reformed Second Helvetic Confession of 1562 states:

*We also do reject the Jewish dream of a millennium, or
golden age on earth, before the last judgment.*

The 41st (of 42) article of the Church of England originally described
premillennialism as *a fable of Jewish dotage.*

Where do the Jews come into all this? Why had
premillennialism been rejected by the Reformers on the basis
of *Jewish* interest? Surely the Jews of the day had no influence
in the Church, they were too busy being persecuted and
reviled. What is the Jewish connection with premillennialism?
Actually there is a definite Jewish connection in later forms
of premillennialism, but these will be talked about a little
later in this chapter. So as not to confuse the two, the form of
this doctrine present at the time of the Reformers is known as
historic premillennialism.

There is a Jewish connection to historic premillennialism. It's
called the Bible. As the chief feature of this doctrine at the time of
the Reformers is the literal 1000 year reign of Christ on the Earth,
this is what they deemed a *bit Jewish* and hence to be rejected.

Here are just two Old Testament passages that probably gave them difficulties over this:

> *In the last days the mountain of the LORD's temple will be established as chief among the mountains; it will be raised above the hills, and all nations will stream to it. Many peoples will come and say, "Come, let us go up to the mountain of the LORD, to the house of the God of Jacob. He will teach us his ways, so that we may walk in his paths."*
>
> *The law will go out from Zion, the word of the LORD from Jerusalem. He will judge between the nations and will settle disputes for many peoples. They will beat their swords into plowshares and their spears into pruning hooks. Nation will not take up sword against nation, nor will they train for war anymore.*
> (Isaiah 2:2-4)

> *The wolf will live with the lamb, the leopard will lie down with the goat, the calf and the lion and the yearling together; and a little child will lead them. The cow will feed with the bear, their young will lie down together, and the lion will eat straw like the ox. The infant will play near the hole of the cobra, and the young child put his hand into the viper's nest.*
>
> *They will neither harm nor destroy on all my holy mountain, for the earth will be full of the knowledge of the LORD as the waters cover the sea.*
> (Isaiah 11:6-9)

Do you see this figuratively or literally? A premillennialist would look forward to a day when Jesus is ruling from the mountain of the Lord and the animal kingdom will be at rest. An amillennialist would see this all as figurative language.

Just after the time of the Reformation a new idea took hold. Some Catholics put forwards the idea that the events described in the Book of Revelation and other places referred to events that actually took place in the 1st Century AD. This is known as *preterism* and we actually read earlier of a partial fulfilment of Jesus' Olivet discourse that seemed to refer to the Roman destruction of Jerusalem. Yet preterism could never hold all the answers because clearly there are events in the Book of Revelation that were never fulfilled at that time, particularly in the later chapters.

Martin Luther and John Calvin may have held to the amillennial view, but also held to a more earthly view of the events of the End Times. Ladies and gentlemen, I give you the *historicists*. These are people of double vision. They fix their eyes both on a period of history and the Bible, particularly the prophecies in Daniel and Revelation and they say, *I can see the connection, I know who the antichrist / beast / man of lawlessness / dragon is!*

Luther regarded the Turks who were conquering Europe in his day and equated them with the locust army of Revelation 9. Calvin, from his observations of the events of his day, regarded the existing pope as the antichrist. Isaac Newton wrote a book, "The Prophecies of Daniel and The Apocalypse", expounding his historicist views. For Newton, the dragon in Revelation 12 was pagan Rome and the events corresponded with persecution in the early Church.

Of course, there's a built-in corrective filter for the views and conclusions of historicists. If history itself proves them wrong, then that's it, we shrug our shoulders and move on. Yet it doesn't stop Christians right up to the present day from conjuring up dramatic scenarios weaved around the events of the day.

Back to the Protestants, there's a group of them who we've met before in our story: the English Puritans. Now these were serious folk, very intense and driven and wholly committed to the Bible, or at least their interpretation of it. For example, some of them were historicists who believed that the Thirty Years war, between the Protestants and Catholics, corresponded to the latter events depicted in Revelation, culminating in the destruction of the papacy and the Turks, and the conversion of the Jews.

Some Puritans, however, started on a different path. They were optimists and believed that, through a revival of the Christian gospel (with themselves at the forefront, no doubt), the World would be conquered for Christ and that they would usher in the 1000 year Millennium themselves, after which Jesus would return. This view is known as *postmillennialism*, with the Second Coming *after* the Millennium and is based on the hope that things are going to continue to get better and better, leading up to this Golden Age, when the gospel (and Christians) would reign supreme. One devotee of this idea was the key American theologian and revivalist, Jonathan Edwards, who saw his own country as a key player in this End Time optimism.

So by the 19th Century we had three completely different understandings of Revelation Chapter 20. The amillennialists, who were in the majority, believed that this referred to the Church age, and the postmillennialists, who were in the minority, believed that things were just going to get better and better, with Revelation 20 describing a time of great revival. The rest of them, the premillenialists, were going to undergo a theological makeover that was going to have significant long-term consequences.

I hinted earlier that there was another later version of premillenialism that had a special Jewish element. This goes by the mouthful of *dispensational* premillenialism, the doctrine ultimately responsible for the *Left Behind* novels and Hal Lindsay's *Late Great Planet Earth*. It's where you'll find the fiercest fighting of this particular battleground. This can be traced back to a single meeting of those who were concerned that the Second Coming didn't seem to figure any more in the thinking of the Church. The time was 4th October 1831, the place was Powerscourt House, Dublin and the people were prominent figures in what was known as the Plymouth Brethren, including a much reviled chap called John Nelson Darby.

At that time historicism was the preferred view of End Time matters, taking the events of Revelation *symbolically* and applying them to current events. Darby disagreed and urged a more Hebraic view of Scripture, reading it, where possible, as a plain, literal account. He advocated a reaction to the looking-back of the historicists and suggested that we look forwards to the future for fulfilment. This was called *futurism*, believe it or not. He took the Scriptures in Genesis and other places, referring to the descendants of Abraham and their earthly inheritance and asked, *so when are the Jews going to receive the fulfilment of this promise? God does not lie, so it must happen eventually.* For Darby this was still in the future and was wrapped up in a series of signposts, not just the return of the Jews to their land but a contentious little word called... the *Rapture.*

Brothers, we do not want you to be ignorant about those who fall asleep, or to grieve like the rest of men, who have no hope. We believe that Jesus died and rose again and so we believe that God will bring with Jesus those who have fallen asleep in him. According to the Lord's own word, we tell you that we who are still alive, who are left till the coming of the Lord, will certainly not precede those who have fallen asleep. For the Lord himself will come down from heaven, with a loud command, with the voice of the archangel and with the trumpet call of God, and the dead in Christ will rise first. After that, we who are still alive and are left will be caught up together with them in the clouds to meet the Lord in the air. And so we will be with the Lord forever. Therefore encourage each other with these words.
(1 Thessalonians 4:13-18)

Darby proposed that the Rapture of the Church, the whisking away of the saints, was just the first stage of Christ's return. Since that time even the subject of the Rapture has split folk into three camps: pre-tribulation Rapture, mid-tribulation Rapture and post-tribulation Rapture – depending on whether you believe Christians are going to catch any of the bad stuff that was going to happen on Earth. It's all very subjective, although everyone can back up their different views scripturally!

Back to the Jews – and read this carefully. One reason why dispensational premillenialism is so contentious is that it's the only

End Time view that really has a positive outlook for the Jewish people, a place in their theology that can properly account for Scriptures such as these:

> *I will establish my covenant as an everlasting covenant between me and you and your descendants after you for the generations to come, to be your God and the God of your descendants after you. The whole land of Canaan, where you are now an alien, I will give as an everlasting possession to you and your descendants after you; and I will be their God.*
> (Genesis 17:7-8)

> *This is what the Lord says, he who appoints the sun to shine by day, who decrees the moon and stars to shine by night, who stirs up the sea so that its waves roar— the Lord Almighty is his name: "Only if these decrees vanish from my sight," declares the Lord, "will the descendants of Israel ever cease to be a nation before me."*
> (Jeremiah 31:35-36)

Without analysing the ins and outs of Darby's new idea, it's enough just to consider that, as the theory makes theological space for the Jews' return as a "special" people, then for those who cannot countenance this possibility, the attractions of dispensational premillenialism are a strict no-no and it's a return to the safe haven of amillennialism. It's back to agendas here, I'm afraid. More of that a little later.

So where are we now? In terms of *prophetic schools*, we have the pessimistic premillenialists – mostly in the USA – as futurists, looking for the signs on their own individual prophetic timetables and confident that things are going to get a lot worse before Jesus comes to make things right. There are the amillenialists – the majority view of the British Church – who take comfort in their preterist views or possibly some historicist ideas, and who shuffle along without too many thoughts about End Times.

Then there are the eternal optimists, the postmillennialists. Where you see people declaring revivals here, there and everywhere then you see postmillennialists, although this movement has birthed new names, exciting names such as *Reconstructionism, Kingdom Now, Latter Rain, Manifest Sons of God and Dominionism.* These are hopeful people who have perhaps allowed their earnest expectations to colour their theological discernment. And that's all I'm going to say on that particular matter.

So many views, movements, theories and offshoots of views, movements and theories! How can a few words of Jesus and (mostly) two Bible books (Daniel and Revelation) generate such opinion and conflict and differences?

I warn everyone who hears the words of the prophecy of this book: If anyone adds anything to them, God will add to him the plagues described in this book. And if anyone takes words away from this book of prophecy, God will take away from him his share in the tree of life and in the holy city, which are described in this book.
(Revelation 22:18-19)

How many are in true danger of these curses? Surely some of them must be, as they can't all be right. Or can they... to a degree? First we must examine ourselves.

How do you view the Bible? How you read the Bible very much depends on your educational and cultural environment and your personal agenda. In other words, none of us is in a vacuum, we are all influenced by others, and how we view End Times in particular is very much determined by our basic agenda. So, for example, those who take a literal view of the Bible would tend to be Christian Zionists, Creationists, futurists and premillenialists. The more liberal Christians would tend to be amillenialists and probably preterists and possibly historicists, or they could view the whole End Time scenario symbolically. Many of today's charismatics, particularly in the USA, would be postmillenialists, though would probably prefer one of the grander names already mentioned.

Doctrines are important to us. Many of us are content to be defined by our Christian labels. *I'm a mid-tribulation dispensational premillenialist* says one, *but I'm an amillenial preterist* says another. Does this mean they are out of fellowship with each other? Hopefully not, but sadly sometimes it does. Some of us are single-issue Christians, defined solely by our label and perhaps even making a career out of it. To them I ask this question – what would happen if suddenly you were convicted of an *alternative* meaning of a foundational Scripture that underpins your label? What would happen if an amillenialist suddenly saw truth in the Scriptures pointing to the Rapture or if a premillenialist was suddenly convinced that Satan is already bound and we are living in the Millennium?

Although this is very unlikely, it could happen. We should always find room for promptings of the Holy Spirit. But my gut feeling is that we would probably ignore such leadings, perhaps even attribute them to Satan, and carry on in our own personal agenda. Does this mean that everyone with a label is a natural *eisegete*, someone who interprets Scripture in the light of their personal agenda? Does this mean that the only true *exegetes* – those who develop their views in the light of Scripture – are those without a label and an agenda? Can those with a label or an agenda be trusted any more to accept the possibility of alternative interpretations of Scripture that may be at odds with their agenda? It's worth thinking about because there could be another way...

In our Greek way of thinking, absorbed through our educational system, logic rules OK. One plus one equals two... always. Every action has a cause... always. *Everything in the Bible can only be looked at in one way*, because that's how we've been taught; it's logical.

Logic is the beginning of wisdom, not the end.

(Mr Spock, Star Trek)

Perhaps old pointy ears had a point. Logic is good, but it's not the be-all-and-end-all. Logic tells us that, in terms of End Time prophetic understandings, only one of the four positions can be right. Either the preterists are correct, or the historicists, or the futurists or those who believe that the whole book of Revelation (as well as much of Daniel and others) are to be viewed symbolically or as allegory. Even among the futurists there are a myriad of prophetic timelines, with an orderly arrangement of all the events that are going to happen. They can't all be correct can they, that's not logical!?

Hebraic thought has a totally different way of looking at the situation. The Greek view has given us prophetic timetables, with a timeline stretching from now to the Second Coming, with points of reference that all need to be ticked off in logical order, determined by one's reading of Scripture. This is the whole premise behind the "Left Behind" books that some have read as if they are holy writ themselves! The Hebrew view, on the other hand, is to concentrate on the *actions* of God in history, whenever they occur and in whatever order.

The Greek view is to say that either you are a preterist or a historicist or a futurist or an allegorist... or none of these if you've never really thought about such things, or are afraid to do so because it's a minefield! The Hebrew view is that you can be all four at the same time, because they are just simply different ways at looking at the same situation. Yes, there is some truth in the preterist view that there was some kind of fulfilment of Revelation in early Church history. Yes, there is some truth in some of the historist views inasmuch as certain events in history were a type or a shadow of future events. Yes, there is some truth in the symbolism used in Revelation and there is some room for allegory. Yes, there is much truth in the futurist views of what is yet to happen as an ultimate fulfillment of the Scriptures regarding the End Times.

The Hebrew mind says, *let's not quibble about the fine print but let's concentrate on the broader sweep, that Jesus is going to return and we need to be ready for that, not in our bickering about who's got it right but in our godly duty to reach those around us before it is too late for them.*

Maranatha (Come, O Lord)… and please, God, we're ready for you!

The War on Error

The battles are still raging, the fighting is fierce and although there are many casualties, there are few deaths. Some, not many, have laid down their arms and crossed sides, but most keep fighting from their entrenched positions. Both sides declare divine favour. *Our battle is for the Lord*, they cry, and that is the saddest thing. Both believe that they hold the truth and are fighting the good fight to defend it, but it is, in reality, a civil war, a war fought between brothers and sisters, who should be linking arms in brotherhood (or sisterhood), not pummelling each other with their weapons of rhetoric and argument.

How the Church lost the Truth is the statement declared in this short analysis of Church history. As surely all Bible believers would agree, the truth is to be found within the pages of that same book. Where better, then, to start our story by looking at folk who actually lived *within* the Book?

The Children of Israel lived their lives by the rules and regulations given by God to Moses on Mount Sinai, the *Torah*. So their understanding of the truth was dictated by these teachings. They were aware of other ideas that were drifting around from the pagan cultures that surrounded them, but God still protected them, using those who were swayed by false gods as a warning to the rest. They knew that they were God's people and lived accordingly to that revealed truth.

These false gods unfortunately were constant thorns in the side of the Jews, as the land was settled and God raised up prophets to steer the folk along a godly path. Perhaps the low point of Old Testament history was the reign of King Manasseh, who openly encouraged his people to follow the pagan entities of Baal, Asherah, Ashtoreth and Molech. The truth was being lost through these frontal assaults and the end result was judgement and the eventual punishment of exile. But, before this, a glimmer of hope presented itself. This came in the form of King Josiah, the young Reformer in the final days of the Jewish Kingdom and the grandson of Manasseh. He rediscovered the truth of God's Word, hidden for so long and supplanted by the lies of the foreign gods.

The Word became flesh and the Truth walked among men. These were the days of Jesus the Messiah and we put ourselves in the shoes of his earliest followers, right after he left them for the very last time. The struggle they had was in coming to terms with the fact that the teachings of their Lord and Master were to take precedence over all they had heard before, particularly the instructions that they had received since they were young, from the oral traditions, supposedly passed down through the generations by word of mouth.

When every one of these Jewish Christians had died, each having contributed to an unprecedented explosion of belief in the risen Christ, this young Christian world entered a new age and everything changed. The truth was no longer clearly visible, because as the Gentile world opened itself up to this new faith in the death and resurrection of Jesus Christ, the flow of traffic was not one-way. The Jewish framework of the faith was slowly eroded by ideas from the Gentile world, mainly from the ancient Greek philosophers, Plato and Aristotle.

We then saw how the early Church Fathers had a job on their hands fighting off heretics such as Marcion and the Gnostics, a task that was made easier by the fact that these battles were usually won using the arguments from Greek Philosophy, the prevailing mindset of the time. Every Church Father except Tertullian was, in fact, a

Christian philosopher and it is easy to see how Biblical truth had a hard time of it, fending off these alien corruptions.

It was largely through the Alexandrian Fathers, Clement, but more particularly Origen, that the Christian faith was so infiltrated by the teachings of Plato that it is hard to see the join between the two. Allegory became the chief tool of Bible interpretation, far removed from the Hebraic methods employed by Jesus and the first Christians, and introduced to the wider Church by Augustine, the Father of Western Christianity.

We then saw the rise of the philosophical ideas of Aristotle, introduced to Thomas Aquinas by Arab and Jewish scholars. Aquinas was the most influential Christian philosopher of the Middle Ages and he did to Aristotle what Augustine did to Plato, integrating his ideas so thoroughly and cleverly into Christian thinking that no-one suspected that anything was amiss. No-one now saw the problem of the Christian faith as an amalgam of Biblical revelation and Aristotelian reason.

The Reformers, led by Luther and Calvin, didn't actually reform as much as you think. They may have rejected Aristotle's rationalism, but they were still partly bound by the Platonism of Augustine, such as in the continuation of State Churches.

Allowing Aristotle into the Church had an ominous fulfilment when those within the Church began to reflect the rationalism and humanism of such secular movements as the Renaissance and the Enlightenment. Christian belief became more and more diluted, even producing groups like the Deists, where God was relegated to the task of the Creator, followed by absentee landlord.

There was a brief respite with the early Methodists, a throwback to the very earliest Church, the great awakenings in America and the missionary movement, but the 19th Century brought a whole swathe of modern day heresies, all throwbacks to the early days of pagan infiltrations. The Catholic Church turned inwards into similar errors. Then there was Christian evolutionism, higher criticism and the rise of liberal Christianity, by which time the rot had really set in for the timeless truths of the Christian faith.

So where has this all brought us to now? Countless thousands of denominations, fringe groups and out-and-out cults, all claiming to be custodians of the truth, as revealed to them by their founders and/or the Holy Spirit.

One Lord, one faith, one baptism... and over 38,000 Christian denominations!

> *I appeal to you, brothers, in the name of our Lord Jesus Christ, that all of you agree with one another so that there may be no divisions among you and that you may be perfectly united in mind and thought. My brothers, some from Chloe's household have informed me that there are quarrels among you. What I mean is this: One of you says, "I follow Paul"; another, "I follow Apollos"; another, "I follow Cephas"; still another, "I follow Christ."*
> (1 Corinthians 1:10-12)

Our current Christian world has enough obstacles to evangelising the World without having to deal with conflicts within. But it is tearing itself apart and the World looks on in sheer puzzlement.

> *If Christians claim to have the truth, how can they not agree among themselves what this truth is?*

We need to get our house in order and to do so we need to get back to basics. Back to the Bible. Not *Bible + the traditions of men* or *Bible + Plato* or *Bible + Aristotle* or *Bible + the agendas of man* but the pure unadulterated Bible of Jesus and the first Christians.

We then looked at the Jewish Bible interpretation methods used by Jesus and the Jews of his day. We looked in particular how allegory, a consequence of Platonism, had been used to obscure rather than illuminate the truth and how sometimes a plain reading of Holy Scripture was, and still is, all that is needed to help us understand what is in God's heart.

We identified five key battlegrounds, doctrinal areas of conflict that have separated Christians ever since the days of the Church Fathers. We looked at them with two thoughts in mind: what was Jesus' own understanding of this and, if Christians have deviated from this, what has influenced them to do so?

The issue of Creation is a thorny place to start. Perhaps the most visible current battles have been over creationism and evolution, often played out in the view of the wider public. Then there is the issue of Israel and the Jewish people, another hot chestnut, but this one borne out of a lengthy shameful injustice played out in the full span of Church history. Getting personal are the issues of personal salvation and the hugely contentious and ignored doctrine of Hell. Huge battles have been fought there, particularly against the backdrop of the modern climate of ecumenicalism, multiculturalism and tolerance. Finally, to round things off, the debate around the issue of End Times and all that entails.

How the Church lost the Truth. It is my contention that all we need to know about this is demonstrated by the key battles fought over Creation, Israel, personal salvation, Hell and the End Times.

There was a time when the Church had *the* truth, but that was a brief time when all Christians had was the direct teaching of Jesus and his apostles and the Hebrew Scriptures to back these up. Somehow between that time and this time, much of the truth (but not all of it, otherwise no-one gets saved!) was lost. To find out what has happened is to simply ask ourselves what has happened between *then* and *now* to that truth.

Hopefully this book has given you some pointers towards answering that question. The Church has been infiltrated from without and within. Although most of the damage has been done by the pagan Greek philosophies of Plato and Aristotle and others, we cannot absolve ourselves from responsibility. Much of the truth has also been lost because of what goes on *within* ourselves. It is down to my much hammered point: *agendas.*

In the way of a review it is now useful to remind ourselves of how each of our key historical characters fared in the various battles, in order to ascertain their agendas. We start with the truth, as in *The Truth*, as in The Way, The Truth and The Life, as in Jesus himself. We can moan about the others that came after him but he is untouchable, beyond criticism and reproach. He was a Six Day young Earth creationist (and Creator), who believed that he was the only way to God and that all who reject him are doomed to eternal conscious punishment in Hell. He believed that there would be a day of reckoning when God would wrap things up and seemed to be a premillennialist inasmuch as things were going to get worse before the End of Days. As for his thoughts on the Jews and their future he didn't speak specifically, so we'll take that as an abstention for now. So what was Jesus' agenda? He spoke much of his mission and identity, but perhaps he summarised it best here:

> *I have come that they may have life, and have it to the full.*
> (John 10:10)

It is fair to say that his apostles, who all gained their theology and practices at his feet, had no reason to diverge from his views. As we don't know what they said and wrote, other than that which became inerrant Holy Scripture, it is inadvisable to query them on that basis. Suffice to say, their agenda would have been to present Jesus to the World, so that folk may have life and have it to the full.

Moving on to the early Church Fathers, who largely viewed their theology through Greek-tinted glasses, we start to see a moving away from the doctrines and beliefs of their forbears. Although their views on Hell and the End Times tallied with the apostles, the same can't be said about other things. For them a belief in Jesus wasn't the only qualification for Heaven, it seemed to be open for Greek philosophers and their rationalist friends too! Creation became subject to their rational approach, although at least God's role in this wasn't doubted. As for the role of the Jews, antagonism had set in and a corresponding theology was being formulated to justify this. So... agendas? At best they were looking for a way to integrate the philosophic ideas from their former life into their new life in Christ. At worst they were attempting to fit Jesus into their tried and tested philosophic systems. We will give them the benefit of the doubt by declaring that the truth is somewhere in the middle, between the two positions!

Not so, the next person in our review. Origen deserves a whole paragraph to himself, so significant was he, although not in any good ways. His position in the battlefield was right at the front, confrontational and effective, wielding the sword of allegory, holding aloft the shield of Plato. His legacy was a devastating one in all five battles. Creation, Israel and End Times were all excused away as symbolic, allowing him to put forwards his own views, laying down the fundamentals of amillennialism, replacement theology and universalism for others later to follow and distribute to the Church at large. His agenda was a thoroughly Greek one, with an attitude that was both sincere and true to his convictions, but with dangerous consequences.

Augustine took Origen's building blocks and packaged them to a wider audience, establishing amillennialism and replacement theology as the party-line of the dominant Church right up to modern times. In matters of Hell and salvation, he followed the traditional line of orthodoxy that had bypassed Origen, but on Creation he fell prey to the Greek tendency of embellishment and the second-guessing of God's intentions, rather than just reading the Genesis account at face value. Thomas Aquinas was much the same, however he over-emphasised the role of sacraments in the Church as means of salvation. The agendas hadn't really changed; it was still the search for an accommodation for the rationalism and allegorical thinking of Greek philosophy within a Biblical framework. But, with the huge influence of Augustine and Aquinas, it was a sense of normalising this agenda as a "Christian" agenda, not to be questioned or queried. Plato and Aristotle had entered Christian mainstream and were free to stride down the main street of Christendom without fear of rejection, a privilege that the Jews of the day couldn't contemplate in their wildest dreams.

Even allowing for Martin Luther's quirkiness over the matters of Israel and the End Times, the Protestant Reformers were in most cases heroes of the battle, fighting mainly under the banner of truth. *Sola Scriptura*, *Sola Fide* and the rest, were their battlecries, with a return to Six Day young Earth Creationism, a more Biblical view of Israel and an insistence of personal responsibility for one's salvation, rather than relying on the sacraments administered by the Church (though many Protestant churches carried on the practices afterwards). Hell was still a place of eternal, conscious punishment; at least that particular doctrine had been held unswervingly (apart from Origen, of course) since the time of Jesus.

Curiously the amillennialism of Augustine was still their preferred view of the Millennium, though post-millennialism made inroads through those über-Reformers, the Puritans. So, although the Reformers had an agenda of good intentions, with their desire to return to a Biblical faith, there were still some Trojan horses in evidence, particularly their sympathetic view of Augustine and, by implication, the Greek philosophy at the heart of his thinking.

Then it all began to fall apart and the battlefields became places of real carnage, with Biblical truth torn to shreds, the Sword of the Spirit no match for the daggers of rationalism, simply because there were not enough warriors willing to bear arms in the battle. Compromise, tolerance and ecumenicalism were the shields of protection for those who had allowed the timeless truths of the gospel to be diluted and even corrupted by the implications of the ideas of Plato and Aristotle.

Creationism was an easy target, such was the growing strength of scientific rationalism in swaying secular minds to *alternative* explanations of our World. The majority of Christians accepted the compromise of theistic evolution, as they broadened the narrow gate, as did the early Church Fathers, to allow more into Heaven, regardless of their actual beliefs and, if some slipped through to the other place, Hell had been re-fitted, to make it less uncomfortable. Although many evangelicals had embraced Christian Zionism of one form or another, most were still bound within the subtle grip of anti-semitism and replacement theology. And End Times had become a battle fraught with extra dangers, on account of the minefields of competing doctrines that crossed the battlefields.

Our agendas, as 21st Century Christians, are as varied as they can be and, as we are now living in the "age of individualism", there are possibly as many agendas as there are Christians! We now have to take into account such modern trends as postmodernism, reflected in the emerging Church movement as well as still having to deal with *hey, listen to me, I have a new revelation* and *hey, listen to me, I've worked things out intellectually and now it makes sense.*

We are complex folk, exposed to such a variety of influences, not least from the media that feeds our minds. Yet, as Christians there are two dominant agendas that define us and inform our beliefs and actions. The primary agenda is always going to be the work of the Holy Spirit, sanctifying us as far as we allow him to, and the secondary agenda is the mindset that supposedly Jesus has rescued us from, the dominant mindset of the Western World of the 21st Century. This is the mindset that undergirds our educational systems, our culture, our media and our communication systems. It is a Greek mindset, fashioned from the rationalism of Aristotle and the dualism of Plato, and is the primary agenda of all who have not been regenerated by the saving faith in Jesus Christ.

It is time for us to think hard of the agendas that we follow. We can see the Greek mindset informing the thinking of Christian teachers from the early Church Fathers onwards. We must decide whether we are going to *go with the flow* or earnestly seek for Biblical truth, *wherever it may be found and wherever it may take me*. Should it be enough for us to accept a teaching simply because my pastor / my favourite teacher / my denomination / the pope / Martin Luther / Augustine / the Church Fathers agreed with it? Shouldn't we always follow Jesus *firsthand*, rather than second-hand through the interpretations of others, some of whom had their *own* agendas when proclaiming their views?

It is time to go one stage further and analyse these agendas to see what lies at the *root* of them. This is where it gets difficult, contentious, even *judgemental*, for some. This is not to judge, however I make no apologies for provoking you. Only God can judge us and ultimately all our interactions with each other, before that awesome day just pale into triviality. So here we go...

If you are swayed by the negative propaganda on Israel and its dealings with its problems, or you are offended by any intimation of Jews as *chosen people*, then the chances are you do not subscribe to any form of Christian Zionism and are most likely convinced of the arguments of the replacement theologians. If this is so then you are following a doctrine borne out of misplaced hatred and justified through the ideas of Plato, rather than the plain narrative of the Old Testament story and the tight arguments of Paul in the central section of the Book of Romans. The root of anti-Semitism is hatred and the root of replacement theology is error. Take your pick.

If you allow secular scientific rationalism to colour your views of Creation then you have allowed others to tell you how to cherry-pick truth from fiction or symbolism, in your reading of the words of the first chapter of Genesis. Every time you read Holy Scripture with a part of your brain saying, *this can't be true, there must be another way of explaining this*, then a little bit of doubt has set in. If you read plain teachings of Jesus, such as "*I am the way and the truth and the life. No one comes to the Father except through me*" but your experience, tolerance or advisors have told you, *of course he didn't really mean this... literally*, then a little bit of doubt has set in.

Views on Hell were more or less the same for 90% of the Church's existence. It has only changed in modern times, since the Enlightenment, when rationalism was on the rise and Biblical certainties in retreat. Any belief in Hell, even for the best of reasons, that is not an eternal situation of conscious torment, is not compatible with the actual words of Jesus. Again I say that, if you read plain teachings of Jesus, but your experience, tolerance or advisors have told you, *of course he didn't really mean this... literally*, then a little bit of doubt has set in.

It is understandable why many Christians flinch from any discussions on End Times, because of the extreme baggage it carries and the unseemly passions it provokes. But it's a doctrine that becomes more and more relevant the closer one gets to it. Examine yourself. If you are disinclined to delve into the Book of Revelation, is it through apathy or fear? If you hold to a set of beliefs, then where did they come from? The amillennialism of Augustine, the extreme and pedantic premillenialism of the "Left Behind" books, or the hopeful masked postmillennialism of the self-proclaimed "prophets" and "apostles"? Dare you read the Scriptures yourself and pray for illumination? Granted, it's not the easiest book to unravel and many have tried, but few have succeeded. Again, consider the roots that can inform these attitudes: error and doubt... again.

Now there may be some of you who disagree with some, or even all, of what I have written in the last few chapters. That is fine, I don't claim a monopoly on the truth, but I do claim that I've done my homework, in the historical analysis provided, to show you where my ideas and beliefs have come from. If I have provoked you in any way then I make no apologies, but simply ask you to consider seriously where your ideas and beliefs have come from. What glasses do you wear when you read the Word of God?

It is time to wrap things up and summarise the summary. In terms of the theme of this book – how the Church lost the Truth – it boils down to the roots of the agenda that informs your personal faith. There was hate, error and apathy but, above all, there was *doubt*.

99.9 percent of this book has been written to show you how the Church lost the Truth. So where's the good news? *You did entice us with the by-line... and how it can find it again, after all.* There's a short answer and a long answer to this.

The short answer is that if Truth is being lost, then the best way of finding it again is to lean towards faith and away from doubt. Start to truly believe in the Bible as the repository for Truth, not as the raw material for a good argument. The best way to attack doubt is to stop doing it and start to believe, by taking that step into the unknown and trust in the divine Person, who has authored the Bible. This is not easy, particularly if the inbred rationalism of the Greek mindset is telling you to question everything you may read in God's Word. *Surely I can't take this at face value? Surely He didn't really say this? Surely I can't trust this text? Surely not everything in the Bible is true? Surely I can't always trust in God? Surely I can't necessarily believe in God?*

This is a progressive downwards spiral, and at every point is driven by Greek philosophy, whether it is scepticism or deductive logic or dualism or whatever. *You are asking me to believe something that I have no evidence for or no experience to draw on or no quantifiable proofs for?*

You are totally right... that's what faith is!

Now faith is being sure of what we hope for and <u>certain of what we do not see</u>.
(Hebrews 11:1)

If this is you, if you feel that God is speaking to you in any way, then it's time to talk to Him, one to One.

If you want a longer answer, then you need to go deeper and enter into an ongoing dialogue with God Himself, allowing Him to illuminate his written Word for you. This is not going to happen overnight, it requires patience and perseverance from both of you, though one party has this in limitless abundance. You should be prepared for an amazing journey of discovery, guided by firm unseen hands, rather than floating aimlessly on a sea of opinion, theory and tradition. And this journey into the heart and mind of God starts with a single step... onto your knees in prayer. Here are some words that you can use.

Father God, you have provided us with the Way and the Truth for us, yet many who have professed to follow You have made it so difficult for the rest of us to really follow you. Please release me from all that clutters, confuses and deceives and guide me into Your Word, the Bible, so that I can become a true person of faith and a witness for You in a World that does not understand you but needs you desperately. Amen.

Epilogue

So what of Theodore Dusty and The Fish People? If they had actually existed then you could at least hope for a less dramatic ending for their adventure than is the norm. The People's Temple of Jim Jones, the Heaven's Gate cult and the Branch Davidians of Waco all ended as mass suicide, as did 778 members of the *Movement for the Restoration of the Ten Commandments of God* in Uganda in 2000. *The Family*, led by Charles Manson, who was influenced by both the lyrics of The Beatles and the words of the Book of Revelation, went on a killing spree.

In every case it all ended in tears, or death, for the perpetrators and victims (and their families) of such lunacy. There has never been a happy ending. These "Bible-inspired" groups led either to the grave, jail or the asylum and will continue to do so for as long as folk blindly and meekly allow themselves to be led by supposed "Men of God".

So where are the true Men of God? Can you imagine what could happen if there was a real, authentic, move of God, fuelled by correct understandings of the Bible (rather than formulae, campaigns and strategies), backed up by prayer and sensitivity to the leadings of the Holy Spirit and led by true servants without a whiff of secret agendas or personal ambition, save for the glorification of the Lord Jesus Christ?

Appendix 1: Recommended Reading

Here are a few books that I think you will find useful, arranged by Sections of this book.

Bible Years

The Bible as it Was, James Kugel, Harvard University, 1998

Unlocking the Bible, David Pawson, Collins, 2003

The Book of Jasher, Cedar Fort, 2006

Church Years

How the Church lost The Way, Steve Maltz, Saffron Planet, 2009

The Final Words of Jesus, Jacob Prasch, St Matthew Publishing Ltd, 1999

The Pilgrim Church, E. H. Broadbent, Gospel Folio Press, 2009

Heresy, Alister McGrath, SPCK, 2009

Jewish Philosophy, Norbert Samuelson, Continuum, 2003

Creeds, Councils and Christ, Gerald Bray, Mentor, 1984

Battlegrounds

The People of Many Names, Steve Maltz, Saffron Planet, 2010

Evolution: A Theory in Crisis, Michael Denton, Adler & Adler, 1985

The Lie: Evolution, Ken Ham, AIG, 1987

In Six Days: Why 50 Scientists choose to believe in Creation, John Ashton, Master Books, 2001

The Road to Hell, David Pawson, Hodder & Stoughton, 1996

Appendix 2:
Now Why Don't You. . . ?

At the time of writing five of my books are still available for purchase, either through Amazon, Christian bookshops or directly from www.stevemaltz.com

How the Church lost The Way... *and how it can find it again*
The story of how the Church has been infiltrated by a pagan virus that has worked its way through every facet of our Christian life and how we can start fighting back.

"*With great insight, explaining many concepts simply, Steve Maltz brings us back to the root of our Christian faith. I believe that every pastor and ordinand in the country will benefit from reading this book.*" Mark Weeden, Senior Pastor, Worthing Tabernacle

The Land of Many Names: *Towards a Christian understanding of the Middle East conflict*
This book has been generally accepted in the UK as the most balanced, well-reasoned and clear explanation of the position taken by those Christians who believe that God still has a purpose for Israel today.

"*This book lives up to the blurb in its style – lively, entertaining and provocative – it gives a well-researched and popular account of Israel's history from the days of Abram to Sharon . . . Addictive,* dented some of my convictions and made me think hard." Tony Sargent, Principal of International Christian College, Glasgow

The People of Many Names: *Towards a clearer understanding of the miracle of the Jewish people*
This book pulls no punches in providing an insight into God's plan for the Jew, Christian anti-semitism and includes practical suggestions for reconciliation within the Body of Messiah.
   "I think it's brilliant, inspired, a great read, of interest to both Jews and Christians, a breath of fresh air – and timely! What more can I say!" Julia Fisher, writer and broadcaster.

Jesus, the Man of Many Names: *A Fresh Understanding from the dawn of time to the End of Days*
Are you prepared for a new book about Jesus that does offer fresh insights without boasting new revelations? Drawing on sources from the Jewish world, ancient and modern, the author will take you on an exhilarating, lively and entertaining exploration of the life and times of the Jewish Messiah.
   "Steve Maltz has a gift for combining pacy writing with crystal-clear distillation of his own careful study of scholarly resources and a firm grip on the Gospel. The result is a fascinating new landscape of insight" David Andrew, editor Sword Magazine

The Truth Is Out There: *The Ultimate World Conspiracy. Who really is pulling the strings?*
Is history just a random sequence of events, or are there secret manipulations? What makes us tick? How did the World as we see it come to be? Read this book if you are prepared to be challenged.
   "Steve Maltz has a rare gift of being able to communicate complex ideas in a way that leaves you thinking that you have read the work of a genius but can still follow his argument clearly. A brilliant read for an evangelist to engage with a sceptic or to give as a gift for 'food for thought' " Tim Leffler, The GoodBookstall. org.uk